BELOW THE BELTWAY

BELOW
THE
BELTWAY

Money, Power, and Sex in
Bill Clinton's Washington

John L. Jackley

Regnery Publishing, Inc.
Washington, D.C.

Library of Congress Cataloging-in-Publication Data

Jackley, John L.
    Below the Beltway : money, power, and sex in Bill Clinton's
    Washington / by John Jackley.
       p.   cm.
    Includes index.
    ISBN 0–89526–476–5 (alk. paper)
    1. United States—Politics and government—1993-   —Humor
    2. Political culture—Washington (D.C.)—Humor. 3. Political
    corruption—United States—Humor.   4. Clinton, Bill, 1946-   –
    —Humor.   I. Title.
    E885.J33 1996
    973.929—dc20   96-7511
                                                        CIP

Published in the United States by
Regnery Publishing, Inc.
An Eagle Publishing Company
422 First Street, SE, Suite 300
Washington, DC 20003

Distributed to the trade by
National Book Network
4720-A Boston Way
Lanham, MD 20706

Printed on acid-free paper.
Manufactured in the United States of America

10 9 8 7 6 5 4 3 2 1

Books are available in quantity for promotional or premium use. Write to Director of Special Sales, Regnery Publishing, Inc., 422 First Street, SE, Suite 300, Washington, DC 20003, for information on discounts and terms or call (202) 546-5005.

This book is dedicated to my children, Julia Anne and Robert Winfield, who have endured so much; to my beloved grandfather Gar, who passed away last year; and to Susan Theresa Lea Courtney, who took me on through to the other side.

CONTENTS

Acknowledgments   ix

Prologue   An Open Letter to Washington   3
Introduction   Low Friends in High Places   9

Chapter 1   Shooting the Wounded   15
Chapter 2   *Homo Politicus* and the Culture of Ambition   31
Chapter 3   Dear Diary   43
Chapter 4   Who Are These People?   51
Chapter 5   Bill Clinton and the Fall of Politics   61
Chapter 6   "You Could Be Mine!"   75
Chapter 7   Money   85
Chapter 8   Sex   95
Chapter 9   Influence   103
Chapter 10   Eggheads and Quote Machines   117
Chapter 11   Annoying Man   135
Chapter 12   The Web   147
Chapter 13   http://WWW.Senate.House.Government.?   165
Chapter 14   The Culture of Clinton   179

Epilogue   195
Index   199

ACKNOWLEDGMENTS

THIS BOOK COULD not have been written without the help, encouragement, and support of many people along the way.

Special thanks go to publisher Al Regnery, whose patience and understanding sustained this book project from start to finish, and to Richard Vigilante and Charlotte Hays, whose editorial direction guided the transition from manuscript to book. I am also thankful to Jennifer Reist, David Dortman, Trish Bozell, and the rest of the great staff at Regnery Publishing for helping to make the book happen.

Thanks also to the Portland State University history community and Drs. Bernard Burke and Jim Heath, and as before, the intellectual and honor traditions of Washington and Lee University in Lexington, Virginia.

Heartfelt thanks to Larry and Jo Jackley, my parents, who were with me every step of the way over the past years, and to my brother Mark and sisters Jill and Anne. Also, thanks to Mike Baskin (the world's coolest brother-in-law) and Stewart Dreschler, who interprets New York to me.

Also thanks to Megan Butler, Slick, Scot and Leah Sideras,

Dave Franks, John Moss, Rick and Kris Beam, Tim and Marcia Van Horn (and Megan and Duncan), Chip and Kathy Martin, Karen Griffith (and Evan and Allyson, who someday will be a fine writer herself), the entire Courtney family, Steve and Anne Cruzen (and the lost ski weekend gang), Penny Peloquin and the Pine Hollow crowd, Connie Garland, Sharon Ringheisen, Chari Smither, Nancy Sullivan, Linda West, Debbie Wuerch, Skeet and Mary Will, Jim and Judith Heath, Jeff and Leslie Kelleher, Mike Freese and Beverly Vernell, Nancy DeSouza, Jim Sellers, Paul Dittman and Ken Brooks, Mark Fryburg and Laura James, Mark Johnson, Rod and Melissa Kuckro, Ted Owen and Kathleen Barneby, Dan and Becky James, Jill Gomery and Mike McFarland, Jeff Nelson, Tony Naegle, Paul and Wai Yee Bonneau, Dr. Russ Dondero, Dr. Paul Drukas, Dr. Marvin Harner, Carol and Ken Barnhart, Sheila and Scott Zachry, Tom and Barb Mildner, John Fund, Bill Gilmore and Vicky Cottrell, Dan and Kate Kelleher, Suzanne Lindsey, Dave Thompson, Scott Smith, and everyone else who provided support and encouragement along the way.

Hats off and a deep bow, please, to Roadtrip. What can I say, dude? You're a star, and I thank you from the bottom of my heart. And thanks, too, to all the sources who needed to stay anonymous, especially those in the White House and the Democratic political, lobbying, congressional, and consulting circles in Washington, D.C. It was deeply gratifying, especially in the case of White House staffers, to see so many who understood that their ultimate loyalty is to the public and the Constitution.

The opinions, judgments, arguments, and shortcomings of the book, of course, are entirely my own.

West Linn, Oregon
February 1996

BELOW THE BELTWAY

AN OPEN LETTER TO WASHINGTON

TAKE IT FROM ME, don't read this book. Make fun of it, dismiss it, smirk your professional smirk and go on. Go ahead, pretend it and the emotions from every neighborhood in America— the feelings on which I draw—don't exist either.

That's OK. Really OK, in fact. Because y'all are in trouble. Real trouble. Deep kimchi, if you catch my drift. Look at yourselves: Do you honestly think the forces that propelled Ross Perot in 1992 and the radical Republicans in 1994 are gone?

Well, think again, Washington; 1992 was just the beginning, and 1994 was only the prelude to the storm. Sure, you might have written off Perot, but he was fundamentally right. It was never about *him*—and the numbers prove it. A *Newsweek* magazine poll in the fall of 1995 reported that only 27 percent of the respondents said they'd vote for Perot—but 52 percent said they'd mark the ballot for Colin Powell. And when Perot went on the Larry King show to announce that he was forming a third party, over 800,000 people called within minutes. The discontent was always about the nation's boiling, visceral hatred toward you and your town—the privileged class, fattened on the public dime—the Georgetown socialites and the pols and the pontificators—from Al Gore to Al Hunt.

And you never catch on. "Never in our wildest dreams did we think voters would actually believe the crackpot," Mary Matalin, the former Bush political adviser, opined in *All's Fair*, the widely promoted "tell nothing" book she wrote with serpent-headed spouse James Carville, Clinton's main man on the strategy front.

(By the way, there's no truth to the rumor of a connection between the proliferation of Washington insiders that reveal nothing and the rise of drug-resistant bacteria.)

The truth is that the voters are wilder than your wildest dreams.

Tell you something else, too. It really isn't about the money, although that, too, has to change, and it's going to.

It's about attitude. Always has been, always will be.

It's the anger we feel when we witness the arrogance of a George Stephanopoulos, at thirty-three a master of cultivating the cult of celebrity—and damn little else—smugly informing us shortly after the voter revolt of 1992 that it was still perfectly OK for Clinton crony Vernon Jordan to work on health care reform while reigning as one of the fattest of Washington's fat-cat lobbyists and pulling down $50,000 a year merely for serving on the board of RJR Nabisco Holdings Corporation—a company with a huge stake in health care legislation.

Our eyes narrow when we get preached at by this punk, a life-long member of the Permanent Political Culture, an image-obsessed person who has never held a job off the government's playground and is famous for his sweet paychecks ($95,000 a year as a thirty-year-old palace guard for House Majority Leader Richard Gephardt, and $125,000 as an adviser for Clinton), free health insurance, expensive haircuts, and even more expensive girl-friends. We resent people of privilege—and the Clinton adminis-tration's stocked chock-full of 'em—from Bill and Hillary and their yuppie Renaissance weekend friends on down. We don't like it when these spoiled Beltway brats lecture the rest of us on what's right for America at a time when it's getting hard for regular folks to make ends meet. They don't know how tough it can be just to pay the rent out here. As *Philadelphia Inquirer* reporters Donald L. Bartlett and James B. Steele put in their book, *America: What Went Wrong?*, "If you work for a living and you are in the middle-class income range... the chances are that your standard of living is falling or will do so in the coming years. If you are striving to join the middle class, you are working against the odds." You Washing-ton types went into a frenzy when the government shut down briefly. You were panicked that those cushy jobs for which we pick up the tab might be threatened. But shaky job tenure is a way of life out here. Millions of Americans are being forced into lower paying jobs. Many have lost a portion of their benefits. "The poverty of middle-class life," writes Jim Wallis in *The Soul of Politics*, "is a sign of crisis."

Our anger rises when it's reported that George Bush doesn't know how a cash register works and doesn't know the price of hamburger meat. (Come to think of it, I'd love to see Clinton's whiz-kid white boys pass the same test—starting with Ira Magaziner, Robert Rubin, Harold Ickes, and throw in Hillary Rodham Clinton, too, for good measure.)

Our resentment takes the form of the hundred thousand "Yeah, FUCK-YOUs" that rose up nightly in living rooms and bars across the country when political action committee (PAC)-addled former House Speaker Thomas Foley solemnly promised "action" on campaign finance reform in 1993 and then did everything within his power to kill it behind the scenes.

It's the explosive fury that men and women of all political stripes and colors feel when Hillary Rodham Clinton starts wagging her finger at them and uses that preachy, moralizing tone of voice that makes fingernails on a chalkboard sound mellow and sweet. (West Wing staffers who work for her husband have taken to using the phrase, "Her Rodham Clintonness.") Most people, in fact, seem to prefer her better when she's merely lying, such as during her pink-suited Whitewater press conference or her explanations about cattle futures profits to a nation where the top 4 percent of Americans make as much as the entire bottom half of U.S. workers—all after having told us throughout the 1992 campaign that the "greed" of the 80s was immoral and that she would make things right for us.

For fifteen years, I participated in the political culture, mostly as a Democratic Capitol Hill press secretary.*

I'm pretty much an outlaw Democrat—like most Democrats outside Washington, I think and say whatever the hell I want and defy the latté-and-Thai-food crowd at the Democratic National Committee (DNC) to do something about it. I like to shoot guns, too, lots of them, and the bigger the better. It's great for scaring the hell out of your liberal friends, especially when you drink tequila. Sometimes I go to the thirty-nine–acre chunk of Eastern Cascade Mountain wilderness I own above the Columbia River Gorge in Oregon and do both with my girlfriend Susan. I'm a better shot but she can hold more tequila, so I figure it's an even draw. Hell, somebody's got to keep up this grand and glorious literary tradition. Big decisions for most writers these days are whether to call your therapist or your lawyer first. Author Hunter S. Thompson used to carry the mantle of the shooting and drinking man of letters, but the word I hear now is that he's tired and old, lost his nerve, and can't shoot worth a damn. I'd challenge him to a duel but I hear the son of a bitch can't see.

---

* I started off lobbying for Jimmy Carter's Panama Canal treaties, jumped to a short-term consulting job, and then snagged my first Hill gig as Congressman Tom Luken's press secretary—an assignment that was like dealing with Hannibal Lecter, without the cage.

Unlike the establishment Democrats, I believe character is an issue and honor is important. I grew up in a family environment marked by strict (by today's standards) Army discipline. Dad was a colonel, Airborne, Special Forces, and my childhood landmarks were studded with names of war—the "Dom Rep" in '65, Viet Nam in '66–'67—and tempered by the liberal religious faith of my mother's Bostonian Unitarian Universalism.

Now I'm on the outside with the rest of America, where your comfort, your finances, and hell, even your survival are not guaranteed by government fiat. I've had my share of ups and downs and hard knocks that are common outside the world of the federal government's paid-and-guaranteed heath care system (the "system"— that's what outsiders call it, the Americans that hover on the margin, hungering for a little piece—just once!—of what you K Street lizards take as your God-given right).

Life outside the political culture has a better edge to it now. The air is cleaner. The path may be narrower, but it's easier to see.

The outside opens your eyes to the rage. There's a lot of it here, and it's aimed at you. That's right—you. Look in the mirror, and what do you see? A red-suspendered, yellow-tied, horn-rimmed, *Washington Post*–toting, late model import car–driving, well-fed man or woman of Washington's privileged class. For you, taxes are an issue to pontificate on at the Palm. But for us, taxes may be the difference between saving and not saving. We're even madder that Bill Clinton—who convinced us he was one of us—has lied to us about a number of things, beginning with a middle-class tax cut and taking the long road home.

Our anger is deep, too. A *Times-Mirror* national survey in September 1994 depicted an America "even more distrustful and hopeless about its government than in 1992," and *Knight-Ridder*'s Angie Cannon reported that "more voters want traditional politicians replaced with a fresh batch." Two-thirds of those polled said Washington needs new leaders. By the fall of 1995, a national poll would reveal that 49 percent of the American people thought the federal government was controlled by lobbyists, 25 percent said the Republicans in Congress, and 6 percent said the president.

Here's something else, too, for you Republicans and conservatives: It's not just Clinton.

We think you all lie, every one of you, from Clinton to Bush to Newt Gingrich. We don't see a whole lot of difference among your supposedly opposing crowds.

See, we're not happy for you and precious "policy" and "process." We're scared. We're scared about ourselves. We're scared for our children. We worry about bills—and not the way you do. We're not worried about our tab at Sutton Place Gourmet—we worry about being able to buy bread at all, and peanut butter, and milk. We frame houses and hold state jobs and deliver pipes and work second shifts on weekends. We read the newspapers and get depressed because sometimes we can't even afford to buy what the clipping coupons from Val•pak are offering that week. A lot of us are less concerned about the details of Paula Jones's sexual harassment lawsuit against President Clinton than we are about the glee at the sight of that big-hair trailer-park girl causing all that grief to your town's suits-and-cigars crowd.

We think about questions, about right and wrong. Objective morality? It's not a quaint concept for us. We worry about real right and real wrong and what to do about the weaselers like you who make big bucks by confusing the two.

So look out, Washington. Stay your course. Keep watching your televised salons. Keep thinking that Michael Kinsley has anything more important to say other than the fact that he needs a swift kick in the ass.

Because the peasants with their torches and pitchforks are gathering around the gates of your city. This book is written for them. The smell of blood is in the air, and it isn't theirs.

INTRODUCTION

LOW FRIENDS
IN HIGH PLACES

IN 1992, BILL CLINTON was promising to be different and the public was responding. Politics was not corrupting, he and his wife claimed, but ennobling. Public service through politics was a sacrifice, but one they had been willing to make. Could the Clintons actually bridge that gap? Was their moral fiber of sufficient toughness to withstand the temptations along the road to the presidency? Once in the White House, would they really change things? I have long been intrigued by the irrational fundamentals of politics, the roil below the surface that poses as policy and process.

The new administration—and more important, the Washington it engendered—would be the perfect test for the Clintons's claims that politics, and their politics in particular, with its claim not only to a higher moral plane but a higher spiritual one as well, was by its very existence ennobling of those who practiced it (that's them) and salvational for the recipients of their politics (that's you).

After all, the Clintons had made some startling claims that could actually be proved or disproved. They would clean up the town, no ifs, ands, or buts about it. They wouldn't do what past administrations had done, and certainly not those dastardly Reagan and Bush administrations, characterized as moral swamps by the Clintons.

An investigation of Washington in the age of Clinton sounded noble enough, but like all good Washington adventures, it came with a decided twist.

"The key to this town," a labor lobbyist told me many years ago, "is low friends in high places."

It was time to look up a few.

• • • •

I ORDERED A BRACING Bombay-and-tonic and listened to the nearby excited jabbering of a latter-day fall of Rome.

It was the high late summer of 1992 in D.C.—the usual stinking, sweaty, humid, miserable climate for which the town is understandably famous.

And the political climate was as surly as the weather. National politics was having a squalid affair with itself as Ross Perot shook the conventional wisdom to its bones. The countryside of public opinion was in flames as editorial writers, candidates, television commentators, columnists, and everyone in the neighborhood laundromat railed against all things Washington. It was the year, too, of scandal, and Congress's hot check problem had reached epidemic proportions. In the executive branch, in Congress, in the lobbying companies and law firms, thousands who owed their political life to George Bush—or more important, their dinner invitations—were in a true state of shell shock, unable to believe that the American public would not reward the victor of the Persian Gulf with another term.

The Bush nobility, on the other hand, political appointees all, was packing its bags for flight or trying to burrow in. One of Washington's bloodier rituals takes place when a new administration of a different party comes to power and tries to ferret out the ancien régime's political appointees, many of whom have quietly converted to civil service. Paul Rogers, one of my former staff directors on Capitol Hill, would explain gleefully how he, as a member of the Carter administration in 1977, had hunted down Ford remnants in the bureaucracies, one by one, either to "fire their asses" or transfer them to Outer Mongolia. The Bush appointees, naturally, were working overtime to find inconspicuous hiding places in the vast federal bureaucracy until such time as Republicans returned to power.

You can't really blame them. Washington is a hard town. Its lifeblood is ambition, and its streets are littered with those who suffered mortal wounds; the path to power is paved with human roadkill. Victims express bitterness accompanied by wistfulness, an almost perverse love for the game despite the often devastating consequences. A huge knot of twisted souls holds the place together, feeding off the government and creating an ethos of weary shamelessness that bows its head to success of any kind, and to hell with the price; Washington believes that price is paid by those you left behind.

The heart of the town is ice, and betrayal becomes love in a town starved for affection.

For the lobbyists and lawyers who stuck around, the really smart money in the big downtown lobbying firms sighed and started tallying up how much they would have to give to the Clinton crowd, and how soon. Scavengers like my buddies around the table at a political watering hole on K Street were licking their chops and trying to figure out where the biggest pile of scraps would land.

"Congress, Congress, Congress," one of them spat to no one in particular. He threw down a copy of the *Washington Post* with disgust. "Reporters. Talk show hosts. Television. Ross Perot. The goddamn public—yeah, let's not forget the huge pile of crap called *We, the People*—seems to think this whole town is nothing but Congress."

My friend Roadtrip—a better description than his given name, believe me—is one of these lawyer-lobbyists, a veritable Moses the Lawgiver. His contempt was borne of years of practical experience in the bare-knuckles trenches of Capitol Hill politics "before I took my practice public." He writes more legislation than most members of Congress, all to the tune of several hundred dollars an hour plus lavish expenses. Roadtrip comes from the world of political consulting—the mercenaries, the political hit men, the fast buck guys who can with equal élan turn out a TV commercial or turn up a damaging videotape. You can tell by the mean twitchings, the darting eyes always scamming for an angle, that his political radar is on high voltage twenty-four hours a day. I was in the business myself for a while, just long enough to learn there was at least one breed of political hackery to which even I didn't aspire.

"Hey, don't knock it," I laughed. "Congress-bashing is good for business." My book about working behind the scenes in Congress, *Hill Rat*, had recently hit the *Washington Post's* bestseller list.

"That's not my point," he argued. "My point is that they have it all wrong." He paused. "Congress, Congress, Congress," he repeated. He took a hit from his beer and peered at me. "Maybe you have it all wrong," he added suspiciously.

"So what?" I joked.

"Because you're the one who's been on TV. You're the one who's supposed to know what you're talking about."

"There's a connection between television and reality? That's a new one." I had just finished my book tour and took his crack as a compliment. "Rumors about my depth are greatly exaggerated," I added. "Sorry to be costing you money."

His expression mutated into a grin. "Hell, we're making more money than we ever did. Our clients think the public is in all-out revolt, and we got half of 'em believing they're on the brink of extinction with only us holding the rescue line."

"And the other half?"

"We're adjusting their billings." Then he turned serious. "But I mean it. This town is a lot more than Congress. Everyone's blaming Congress for everything. It's not fair."

"Life is unfair," I said in my best Jimmy Carter drawl.

"Don't be a jerk. I'm not saying they don't deserve the rap. But it's for the wrong reasons. There's something deeper at work here."

"He's right," my other friend said excitedly as his spectacles fell to the tip of his nose. "The poll numbers have swung dramatically against not only the Bush administration but also Washington, D.C., as a whole—the entire political culture is under attack."

My other buddy, Datahead, as his friends call him affectionately, is entirely the creation of the computer revolution. As one of Washington's better-regarded pollsters and public opinion experts, Datahead is courted by Washington's political luminaries. "If it wasn't for computers," Datahead once observed cheerfully, "I'd be somewhere back home fixing toasters." Personally, I doubt it. Take the glasses. Datahead doesn't need them—they're clear glass—but he figures they're as handy an academic credential as a Ph.D. He knows what works.

Datahead does one thing: numbers. He handicaps the races, identifies strengths and weaknesses, and discovers how to turn a chink in an opponent's armor into a political San Andreas fault. He decides which lines work best on TV, and with what demographic groups. He cuts the seer's traditional figure: unruly dress, even unrulier hair, skin that rarely sees the sun, and a diet of diet soda and junk food.

And, like any good prophet, he trades on the future but makes sure to get paid before it actually arrives.

"So what's your beef?" I asked them.

"The soul," Roadtrip replied mournfully.

"The soul?" I thought I'd heard it all. Not to doubt my friend, but Roadtrip is legendary in certain circles for alcohol consumption, the alleged land-speed record for the Friday night run to Rehobeth Beach, Delaware, flashy women, and expense accounts the size of November. Matters of the soul are rarely his first choice of conversational gambit; we have all pretty much dismissed his claims to have seen God several times as nothing more than the usual run-of-the-mill ecstatic weekend vision.

"The soul of this town, man. They're not coming close." Roadtrip looked serious.

Then Roadtrip challenged me:

"Find the soul of this town." He seemed to imply I couldn't do it.

I was halfway into my second heaven-and-tonic, and I grabbed the challenge like the red scarf of Pamplona. "The hell I can't," I announced. I stood up and demanded loudly, "Anyone in this joint thinks I can't find the soul of this swamp?"

I looked around and no one, of course, was paying any attention whatsoever. The noise and the bustle had nothing to do with it. I saw a smoky tableau of lobbyists, power brokers, and the occasional elected or appointed official sprinkled amidst the clink of cocktail ice and scanning the horizon for sex. A Bush appointee was peddling his wares to a trade association official to my left, and a well-known journalist was off in a corner, no doubt polishing a puff piece on Bill Clinton. The Washington press corps had already made the quiet collective decision early that Clinton would win, and they'd started pimping for access early.

I chuckled, but I also reminded myself that the inner child of the Permanent Political Class carries a switchblade.

Then it came to me.

"A political Theory of Everything!" I blurted out suddenly.

CHAPTER ONE

SHOOTING THE WOUNDED

And Congress's image has suffered, because, members think, journalistic ethics and standards are not as good as they used to be.
— House Majority Leader Richard Gephardt
in the *New Yorker*, 12 September 1994

Congress is not corrupt. Congress is not on the take. Congress is incompetent.
— Senator Ernest Hollings (D-S.C.)

Is Congress for sale? Hell, I'd be happy if the sons of bitches would just stay rented.
— Roadtrip, early 1995

NATIONAL AIRPORT fell rapidly behind the window of my cab as we crossed the 14th Street Bridge in late September 1992. I looked up at the pigeon-infested monuments on the other side. I sighed. Back again.

• • • •

SEPTEMBER 1, 1992, a few weeks before. "Hey, buddy," the voice on the other end from across the country said with its dangerous trademark chuckle. "What's going on?"

"Stew!" Calls from my friend we'll call Slick, the Washington, D.C., producer of the top-rated tabloid television show *Inside Edition*, were always welcome. I had worked with him on a story in May about congressional perks, and he was a superb source for the more shadowy aspects of life in the nation's capital. A former investigative reporter for Jack Anderson, Slick has fabulous connections that are exceeded only by his taste for extreme downhill skiing. Slick is analytical, sharp, great with people, and motivated, pushed by a populist outrage against official corruption in all its various and manifold forms. I often told him he was wasting his time in journalism and ought to go into politics himself.

"Are you up for a big one?" he asked.

I laughed. *Inside Edition* is the syndicated world's number one show with huge budgets and an audience of fourteen million people. A big one by their standards could be an adventure of truly epic proportions.

"Let's hear it," I said.

Slick went straight to the point. "You know all these Senate and House members that either got beat or decided to retire because of scandals? The word on the street is that these guys are willing to do anything to get another job and stay in town."

"Anything?"

"Anything we ask them to do, natch."

"Natch," I said as a grin quickly worked its way across my face.

"The old bait and dangle, buddy," he continued, "the old bait and dangle. A classic sting. We ask them to do something really outrageous in terms of violating the public trust, offer them a job in return, and see what happens."

"Use a P.O. box," I suggested. "Otherwise they'll be breaking down your door, and we'll need to sell popcorn and tickets."

"Better than that," he replied, and gave me the pitch. "Posing as lobbyists, perhaps under assumed names, we approach retiring congressmen in an attempt to have them place bogus bills in the hopper or submit some inane comment for the *Congressional Record. Inside Edition* will set up telephone answering services to handle our East and West Coast offices. Letterhead, stationery, maybe even promotional pens will be manufactured for the purpose of the sting."

I was rubbing my chin and already thinking of the possibilities. The audience size and makeup were appealing because we could reach the average person on the street and tell them something important about the way Washington really works: that entrenched corruption has become not special but ordinary.

Hmmm. It was also a chance to slap around the elitism and snobbery of the chattering classes of the Beltway and their smarmy groveling at the feet of those in power. (Their argument: anyone not as corrupt as they are has no legitimate right to an opinion.) Being able to show Washington's political culture at its rawest, most honest level, unfiltered by those who make their living collecting the bones thrown to them by the big boys—wow, I thought, something like that doesn't come around often.

I was also trying to figure how in the world I was going to start the search for the soul of Washington that Roadtrip and Datahead had instigated. This seemed as good a starting point as any.

Besides, as Roadtrip pointed out longingly, when I called him, it sounded like one hell of an adventure. "The opportunity to accompany a national television show exposing congressional corruption would be too great to resist," he said.

"Okay," I said, "you do it."

"Hell, I make my living off that kind of corruption," he laughed.

"No," I replied, "You *are* that corruption."

I agreed to let him know when to the stay out of the way. "By the way," Roadtrip added, "your friend Slick is right on the mark. Keep pushing. You never know what you'll find." Our conversation ended. Roadtrip likes to live in a lot of different universes. I live in one of them. We have known each other for a very long time and have slain many demons together, and we have a deep understanding not to betray.

Then I got nervous. Could we really do this *Inside Edition* deal— could we actually pull it off? I'd just written a book titled *Hill Rat* that kicked the stuffing out of the Democrats on Capitol Hill, and

I had appeared on quite a few shows. You had to consider the odds of being recognized, the role of accident, and a host of other factors that can impede an undercover job.

I took comfort in the fact that Hunter S. Thompson once said that television was a long cheap plastic tunnel where the evil run free and the good die like dogs. Hell, I figured, looking back over my years as a Capitol Hill press secretary, I guess that means I have half a chance.

"Let's do it," Slick urged in his next phone call.

"Let's do it," I replied.

In for a dollar, in for a dime.

Sigh. So many politicians, so little time....

By the third week in September, Slick was moving along with the sting and wanted me to come to Washington. Things were jelling, and I was getting amped for the scam and worrying about what could go wrong. Politics is a lot like surfing: it has a real hard impact zone. That's where the fifteen-foot bad boys at Pipeline take you within an inch of your life on the razor edge of the reef, wave after wave after wave. We were going to play in Washington's Pipeline, and it wasn't a game for children. Sneak into town, set the big boys up, snatch the prize, ride the wave, and get the hell out of the way before the whole thing comes crashing down on top of us.

• • • •

THE CAB TOOK ME to Slick's office on Capitol Hill. It was great to see him again. He was wiry and intense with red hair, freckles, glasses, in his mid-thirties, very soft-spoken, easy to work with. We went over the plan, worked on getting our stories straight under our new identities, and agreed to meet the next morning.

The first thing they did was to "gray me up" because I had appeared on their show four months before, and Slick was worried the members might recognize me. Makeup artist Kim Foley added gray coloring to my hair and eyebrows and aged me to from mid-forties to early fifties. They filmed the makeup session itself, which meant Kim and I had to do take after take with a lot of gray gunk.

To fit us into Washington's political culture, Slick had set up a fictional trade association called the National Association of Bolt Distributors, which purported to represent importers and distributors of bolts and fasteners. According to the scenario, the association was very concerned about a government crackdown on counterfeit bolts, which in real life was an enormous problem and the subject of ongoing federal criminal investigations.

(Note: This becomes highly significant at thirty-three thousand feet in a jetliner whose engines are attached to its wings by these bolts. A bad bolt here is generally bad news all around. A two-scotch flier myself, I took the matter personally.)

So that no eyebrows would be raised, we would play it safe and use Washington's standard money-for-influence pitch: offer retiring members of Congress the prospect of employment, and then give them the opportunity to use the powers of their office to earn that employment via a statement in the *Congressional Record*, a floor speech, or other type of official intervention.

It wouldn't be difficult. Slick had found a real proposed federal regulation that would make it tougher to sell counterfeit and substandard bolts in the United States "The object," Slick explained, "is to get the corrupt members to react."

We had a plan. Now we needed the talent. Slick brought in a veteran reporter named Matt Meagher, who using his own name would pose as an importer. Matt had set up a front office with a telephone for "New England Mechanical Trader's Inc." in Woburn, Massachusetts, in case anyone called to check on our bona fides. As Slick's plan read, "Matt should act like he knows little if anything about how Washington works, including asking the congressman if he can't just write a bill to logjam all this stuff. He vehemently opposes this regulation because it will be expensive as hell to test bolts and certify them as adequate before he sells them."

I had a role in the script, too, and it read like a bad novel: "Going under the name Don Lee, John is our executive headhunter from the firm of Lee, Harris, and Carlson. Don Lee recently set up a temporary Washington office to help Matt find a lobbyist in Washington. When Matt asks a question like 'Can't you just write a bill?' Don talks him down to earth and suggests that the congressman merely enters comments in the *Congressional Record* or perhaps file comments on the proposed regulation. Matt met Don because their wives went to school together. Don's business partner, Mr. Harris [Slick], works out of the West Coast mostly, and his other partner, Carlson, is dead."

The undercover taping was to take place in public places only, such as restaurants. Matt would be hardwired with a tape recorder inside his jacket pocket and the microphone hidden in a tie tack or breast pocket (FCC rules precluded the use of a wireless mike).

What were our odds for success?

Well, it wasn't like we had invented the whole scenario out of thin air. The *Washington Post* had just carried a story headlined, "On Capitol Hill, the Search for a Soft Landing." It had detailed the scramble for jobs by retiring House and Senate members—and how difficult it was becoming this year. Datahead had passed on some recent field data from races all over the country, and it looked as though the ranks of the already announced retirees were about to receive some involuntary increases. The used-member market had cooled off considerably in light of an expected oversupply, so we figured we had at least an even chance.

Letters were messengered on our headhunter stationery on September 23 to all retiring members; we didn't want to target any of them unfairly. The letter contained typical Washington pitch ("Congratulations upon the eve of completing a successful 102nd Congress. And special congratulations, too, for completing a rich and distinguished career. History will have its eye on your contributions to our nation's well-being… "). We dangled the prospect of a job, and said we would call soon.

The first bite displayed Washington's morals at their finest. Robert Hartwell, administrative assistant to retiring Rep. Richard Schulze (R-Pa.), called to inform us that he had intercepted the letter, knew from his heart that the congressman wasn't up for the job, and in the same breath offered his own services instead. We all laughed when we heard the tape and arranged to meet him promptly.

As a staffer, Hartwell was not a big enough target on his own to warrant a wake-up call on national television. But we figured he would be a good dry run, so we agreed to meet him at a downtown restaurant.

The mechanics went flawlessly. Steve, our undercover camera operator, set up shop unnoticed at a table across the room, his camera hidden in a briefcase. He quickly zeroed in on us and Hartwell, who had us feeling sorry for him right off the bat because he was so pathetic and disgusting at the same time. Dressed for success in a sharp pin-striped suit, white shirt, power tie, and an attitude to match, he kept reminding us that we should hire him because "staffers do all the work, not the members. They write the laws, do the *Congressional Record* statements, issues the press releases, all that stuff." He was more than happy to put his influence and contacts to work for the right price, but to his credit he pointed out that he could not do anything until he left congressional service.

I watched him strut his Hill Rat stuff and thought, you are so common, so credentialed, so Washington. Ethics in Powertown creates a Marquis of Queensberry fantasy. You can sell out, but it must be at precisely the right time, under the right circumstances, and only according to the rules.

(And cash in he did: Hartwell is now the director of political affairs and senior lobbyist at the American Health Care Association.)

Small fish aside, the major target soon materialized: U.S. Rep. Bob Davis, one of the House of Representatives' more prominent bottomfeeders. He leaped on the offer like a hound in heat. Davis had announced his retirement shortly after being exposed as one of the House's top overdrafters of checks in the now-infamous House bank. He had become briefly famous several years before when his then-wife Marty posed in a see-through black bodysuit for *Time* magazine to prove that not all congressional wives were frumpy. Davis was no stranger to the money-for-influence game. In his previous election, he had shaken down the political action committee crowd for a cool $242,224.

I spoke with him several times on the telephone before our meeting, which was a dinner at the Prime Rib restaurant on K Street, a favorite lobbyist watering hole. Davis had been panting on receipt of the letter and bombarded us with telephone calls to get in on the action. Yes, we were serious, I kept saying. Yes, the money is as good as we mentioned. Yes, we wanted some help, and soon.

In preparation for the meeting, I found myself in a room at the Hyatt, surveying a scene right out of *I-Spy*. Steve sat on the bed, surrounded by open aluminum suitcases full of video surveillance equipment. Matt Meagher was cursing softly in the bathroom and trying to get a good fit for his taping equipment. Slick and I were rehearsing our background stories, our patter, our rap, and trying to assuage Matt's nervousness. "I've done the mob before," Matt kept saying. "I'm not scared of the mob. But these politicians are fucking crazy."

We gathered at the Prime Rib, a place in which the average American will never find her- or himself. The accent is heavy and dark, with lots of ebony and brass. It is a carnivore's lair and not just because of the beef on the menu. The joint teems with lobbyists, members, would-be and actual power brokers, and influence peddlers of all stripes and kinds. Its clientele is overwhelmingly white, middle-aged, blonde-accompanied, overweight, and overlawyered.

I met Mr. Davis as he entered the establishment. "Hey, Congressman, Donald Lee," I said, introducing myself. I was somewhat nervous—would he recognize me? Was the graying-up realistic? Were Slick and I completely out of our minds?

We sat down and ordered drinks. I explained our headhunting firm, and Matt described in detail the burdensome regulations with which bolt dealers must contend.

Congressman Davis soon dominated the conversation, going on and on about how he had already figured out a way around the ethics laws and who he could talk to even though he couldn't lobby his former colleagues for a year after leaving Congress. "[House Majority Whip and fellow Michigander] Dave Bonior has already agreed to help me," he bragged. Davis also made some great comments about PACs, the role of campaign contributions, the purchase of access, and what it took to succeed in Washington.

The congressman's love of the culture of influence was matched by boorish table manners. He became more excited as the talk progressed, eating and talking at the same time (he knew the menu at the Prime Rib so well that he had decided upon the pork chop before arriving). You could almost see the drool of greed begin to form at the edges of his mouth. We had offered him a fantastic job—great pay, benefits, travel, the whole works—and he was beside himself with desire. For one of the largest congressional check-overdrafters in the House, it was unparalleled. Davis represented Michigan's Upper Peninsula, and he candidly told us that after fourteen years in Washington, there was damn little that interested him back home.

Then trouble struck.

The maître d' walked up to the table, stiffly and unannounced, and handed Davis a note. Davis appeared to have trouble reading it. He kept staring at the note, looking and blinking. He would not make eye contact with us.

Matt took it out of his hand.

"What's it say?" Davis asked.

Matt appeared floored for an instant. The note read: "Rep. Davis—the couple across the room with the gift box on the table have you on a secret camera. Be careful."

"What's it say?" Davis asked again. Matt is flailing at this point. His eyes dart. He doesn't reply. Davis asks yet again. Finally Matt blurts, "It says, uh, the couple across the room… uh… wants to buy you a bottle of champagne!"

Matt, stressed and furious, approached Steve's table. "What the fuck's going on?" he whispered.

Steve, the surveillance expert, was at the table with Slick's wife, who posed as Steve's date. The camera was hidden in a gift box on the table. Steve said something to Matt I couldn't hear.

"Get the fuck out of there!" Matt hissed to them, and returned to our table.

Rep. Davis suddenly grabbed the note from Matt. He read it aloud.

His face went ashen. He was silent. "His whole life passed in front of him," Slick chortled later. "He was that close to losing it."

"Oh," Davis said finally. "Oh. It must be some kind of joke. My wife is in the other room at a reception. I bet she did it." And with that, he abruptly left the table to look for her.

I felt a rising sense of UH-OH, kind of like when the cockpit voice prompter in a commercial airliner announces "terrain" the instant before a crash, as Matt told us quickly what was going down. Our voices cut back and forth: "What are we going to do— hold tight—blow this joint—"

Davis returned and said he couldn't find her. We started to wind things down quickly. We gulped our drinks. A lobbyist appeared and said hello to Davis. He was a former staffer for Davis, and he was trying to pull Davis away from our table—physically pulling him, grabbing his coat sleeve and tugging.

Then a waiter appeared and asked us about the "strange couple" across the room. Matt said loudly that yes, they were strange, but now they were gone.

Yeah, the waiter replied, and then added something about a hidden camera on their table.

Matt, Slick, and I exchanged quick glances: Time to boogie.

"Congressman," I said, as if nothing out of the ordinary had happened, "I think we've made great progress here. We're interested, and I hope you are. Let's sleep on it and talk tomorrow."

Fine, Davis said, looking dazed. When he turned his back to the table, I snatched the note and stuffed it into my pocket.

As we reached the foyer of the restaurant, Matt and I overheard the hatcheck woman saying that the manager had called the police. By this time, a crowd of drunken lobbyists had formed around us, giving us the eye and muttering into their gins. I started mentally to calculate which suit I was going to deck first if push came to shove. We didn't know how much they knew, and we weren't going to stick around to find out.

We elbowed our way outside through the glares. I hurriedly shook Davis's hand and said I'd call him tomorrow.

Wasting no time, I grabbed the keys from the valet as Matt and I raced across K Street and into my rental car. Slick jumped in the door. We roared down an alley just as flashing police car lights appeared down the block. I don't remember much about the conversation over the next few minutes, but it was 99 percent profanity.

We regrouped at the Hyatt bar. The waitress approached. "Liquor," I ordered with more than a slight air of desperation, "strong and fast." To release the stress, we all started laughing belly laughs at our close call, even though we knew the entire project was doomed.

Matt then proceeded to tell us that he thought the lobbyist who stopped by the table early into the dinner might have heard him rewinding his tape recorder in the men's room.

"What gave it away?" I asked.

"Oh, I don't know, maybe it was the sound of Davis's voice coming out of the crapper," Matt snapped, then laughed nervously again.

"I don't think so," Steve said with more than a slight degree of guilt in his voice.

We asked how he knew.

Well, Steve explained slowly, he couldn't get the camera to aim properly.

What did he mean?

"Which word didn't you understand? I couldn't get the fucking camera to aim properly."

"So what did you do?" I pressed.

Well, he replied sheepishly, he got up and took forks off an entire row of tables and stuck them under the gift box that hid the camera—just to get a better angle, of course.

We collectively put our faces in our hands, but couldn't stop laughing. Time for reinforcements. "More drinks," I yelled at the waitress, "and fast again."

"And who would be sitting right next to us while all this is going on," Steve continued plaintively, nearly in tears and unable to understand why the rest of us are laughing so hard our sides hurt, "but two Republican political assholes, who watched the whole thing unwind in front of them."

"And then sent the note via the maître d'," Slick said with dismay.

"And then sent the note via the maître d'," Steve repeated.

"FUUU-AACK," Matt groaned. Then he chuckles. "And can you believe that waiter? I gave the son of a bitch a $100 tip, and he still screwed us by calling the cops."

"Typical Washington," I cracked. "Take your money first, and then stick it to you."

"And now Davis has the fucking note," Matt lamented.

"No he doesn't," I replied, handing it to him. "Here's one for your scrapbook."

Reality set in with the third round of drinks. Hell, we figured, the whole thing had been blown completely. Matt was getting nervous about dealing with politicians again and was threatening to get the hell out of Dodge. I mentally rechecked my plane schedule.

The next morning arrived with equal astonishment.

Despite having been told exactly what was going on, despite seeing a hidden camera with his own eyes, despite seeing his professional life flash before his very eyes the night before, Representative Davis left a voice mail message that he had gone ahead and "taken the initiative" to set up a meeting for us with the attorney and regulator who was writing the bolt regulations standards at the National Institute of Standards, and even more, offered to set up a meeting with Vice President Dan Quayle's Council on Competitiveness.

"Taken the initiative!" I shrieked to Slick.

"So Davis is so high on greed," Slick shook his head with amazement, "that he has consciously willed reality away."

Cool. One down and in the can.

"Plus we have another problem," Slick added.

"What's that?"

"Matt's split. He left town already."

"What?!"

"Yeah, it's that politician thing again, I think. Don't worry. I'll work on him. He'll be there when it counts."

"Okay," I replied, relieved. "I'll keep stringing along Davis, but we've got another live one on the line."

South Carolina Rep. Robin Tallon had been right behind Davis in taking the bait. Tallon, however, had loftier ambitions, with an eye on the expected retirement of Ernest Hollings and a wide-open Senate race in 1996. The association position we offered him would be a perfect launching pad: keep his fingers in the Washington game, make some good bucks for a couple of years, stay in touch with the political money boys, then move back home to join the fray.

And if for some reason Hollings didn't retire, well, hell, a quarter mil a year plus perks seemed like a pretty good thing to old Robin for schlepping nuts and bolts.

Tallon was a Southern good old boy's good old boy. He spoke with a heavy Southern drawl and had the reputation of being clever, but no rocket scientist.

"On the other hand," Roadtrip reminded me, "he raised a couple hundred grand in PAC contributions, so his circuits must have clicked somewhere." Tallon had married his secretary in the South Carolina legislature, and the two were regulars at the Democratic Club, the main watering hole for House Democrats.

(My former boss, Rep. Ronald Coleman, had also married his secretary from the Texas legislature, dumped her, then one-upped Tallon by marrying the bartender at the Democratic Club, thus ensuring himself, in the words of our staff director, of a virtually nonstop supply of free liquor.)

Beyond Davis, though, we had another problem—time. The congressional session was almost over, and members were already beginning to head home. We traded calls with Tallon's office until we finally arranged for a brunch meeting the day before the session was expected to end.

Tallon was all grins and mush-mouth as we sat down to talk business. He was charming, witty, smooth—the complete antithesis of the bumbling Davis. Tallon also told us in no-nonsense terms that if our association ever wanted power and influence in Washington, we needed to set up a political action committee and start handing out money.

"Money is the mother's milk of politics," Tallon crooned over his orange juice.

Matt, who had returned, gave him our standard pitch, and we immediately became nervous. Tallon, unbeknownst to us, had been involved in the construction industry in the past and had a good working knowledge of international trade—not to mention nuts and bolts. He was careful, we noticed, to remember our references and contacts, and seemed interested to the point, in our judgment, of being at least as helpful as Davis.

Unfortunately, it didn't turn out that way. Tallon returned to his office and started checking out Matt's references immediately. The first one was the real company in Massachusetts, where the secretary was supposed to answer, "New England Mechanical Traders."

Tallon dialed the number.

Inside Edition, the secretary crooned, completely confusing instructions.

Tallon freaked out and scrambled, working the phones in a frenzy, calling the headhunter's office repeatedly with demands to talk to Donald Lee (who by this time was safely in Oregon, the sting postponed because Congress had left town). Having no success, he called *Inside Edition* and learned that a Matt Meagher actually was there.

Then someone—maybe Tallon, maybe a leak in our Hill intelligence network somewhere—tipped off the Capitol Hill newspaper *Roll Call* and a skewed version of the blown sting turned into headlines for weeks and created wild speculation about the identity of Donald Lee.

"There's a fucking lynch mob out for this guy," Roadtrip called from just off the House floor, yukking it up at my expense. "The gossip in the cloakroom is wild—some of these guys are thinking it might even be a former member or the FBI. They're still scared shitless about ABSCAM, and that was fifteen years ago. Anybody who's ever had an enemy is looking over their shoulder and blaming them for it, right or wrong."

"Mostly wrong," I said.

"Maybe not," Roadtrip replied. "Truth in this town is representational, not specific. If somebody fucked you in the past, this isn't a bad reason to nail them back."

You gotta love this town.

"By the way, I told Datahead everything," Roadtrip continued. "He thinks it's a hoot. We agree that your quest has had a most excellent beginning."

"I'll wait for the check," I said, and we hung up.

CHAPTER TWO

HOMO POLITICUS
AND THE CULTURE
OF AMBITION

*I think people have begun to get the feeling that Clinton might, just conceivably, have
the wit to put together a program that will make us really move as a country.*
— Veteran Democratic Washington hand Harry McPherson,
5 November 1992, in the *Washington Post*

*Did Harry really mean it, or did he want to be the first to jerk Clinton off
in the* Washington Post?
— Roadtrip, 5 November 1992, later that day

WHO IN THE HELL, you might ask, would be crazy enough to
want to work for Bill Clinton?

It might be hard to believe here in 1996 with a wide-open presidential campaign under way, but there once was a time when people
wanted—actually *wanted*—to work for the Clinton administration.

There was a time, believe it or not, when Washington's political
crowd thought that working for Clinton would be good for their
resumes. What we're seeing today, of course, are the makings of
another generation of *desaparecidos*, the disappeared ones, the real
tough political cookies who, if you examine their bio sheets (the
really cool crowd doesn't use resumes but "bio sheets") closely, you
will find there are unexplained gaps of twelve to twenty months in
their employment history. No one is ever "unemployed" in Washington; one is a consultant. Now most of them are consulting all

right—with their favorite bartender, drug dealer, or best friend's spouse.

"So what were you really doing?" you might ask if you cornered one of them at a cocktail party.

Their eyes would dart, and they'd grope for words as they desperately tried to figure out How Much You Know.

They'd try to brazen their way out of it at first, but their explanations would get weaker and weaker: "I was writing a novel... a deckhand on a freighter to Thailand... growing my own vegetables for a new diet I was going to market...."

But you wouldn't let them off the hook so easily. And you'd nail 'em cold. You'd intrude deeply into their personal space until the hair on the back of their neck kissed the wall paint. You'd peer dangerously at them, arch your eyebrows, and in your best "j'accuse!" tone of voice you'd cut them down in a full clip burst: "I know you!" you'd exclaim loudly enough for everyone to hear. "You were the deputy assistant to the second deputy to the cabinet secretary in the Carter administration!"

They would curse you to the end of their days for scraping off the scab of a wound to their careers so deep, so hideous they had decided to pretend it just didn't exist. True survivors like domestic policy assistant Stuart Eisenstat got away with it on grounds of a manufactured "noblesse oblige": they tried their best but just couldn't get that Georgia cracker/Arkansas traveler to understand how things worked in Washington. The observation is normally accompanied by a heavy sigh, the most pronounced of which is the "Eisenstat sigh," which is part of the town's political lore.

And so it will be with Clinton après le déluge, believe me.

But in 1992, when every Ozark cousin-thumper thought that not only was he related to President Bill but that he also ought to work for him, too, the rush for White House jobs was intense. The *Washington Post* published the day after Clinton's election (as it usually does) the "Plum List"—the 3,500 appointments every new president gets to fill. Democratic-leaning Washington players had been sharpening their political razor blades for months—even years. The real players knew that the list for those kinds of jobs had only a handful of names on them, and the competition already was essentially closed. But as one Beltway would-be put it so fondly, "A guy can hope, can't he?" Besides, politics is a wonderful spectator sport as well as a participant one, and one of Washington's greatest rituals is the ongoing buzz by which one compares one's potential performance to that of the incumbent for any given job, and usually favorably.

No one ever compares himself to Bill Clinton. There is an axiom of current thinking in the political culture that any fool can govern better than the First Graduate Student, and probably will.

But this was the dawn of the Clinton age when "government" was still a three-syllable word, and not "gubmint" and preceded by the normal "goddamn." In fact, one of Bill Clinton's enduring legacies will have been the creation of two classes in American society. The minority believes in "gov-ern-ment" and tells you what it does for you. And the majority, who disdain "gub-mint," and can tell you what it does to them.

Once upon a time, way back in late 1992 and early 1993, back when the age looked bright for the young president and his smarter-than-thou wife, back when the newspapers gushed over themselves in praise for this couple that would transform Washington and the world to their liking, people wanted to work for the Clinton administration. And for them as well as for the president, no single time frame would so clearly reveal the relationship between Bill Clinton and the Fall of Politics than the perilous road from Inaugural Day to the hellish fire of Waco, Texas, six months later. It was a time that defined the young Clinton presidency with a series of self-inflicted political body blows from which it has yet to recover—the botched nominations, the betrayal of the pro–middle class agenda he articulated in the campaign, and the spiritualitymongering that culminated in Hillary's white-cloaked appearance on the cover of the *New York Times Magazine*, titled "Saint Hillary."

The administration's ambition was undercut by its arrogance and elitism. It was a time, more than anything else, when the nation learned the hottest flames burned not in cult leader David Koresh's compound, but in the naked ambition and appetite revealed by the president and his followers. These were not people who offered salvation to America, but those separated the most from the whole. And before they were done, this crowd that was so smart, so credentialed, so brilliant, and oh-so-spiritual would preside over the Democratic party's biggest domestic disaster of the twentieth century.

Datahead reported that the early poll numbers—so vital to Washington's corridor hustlers—right after the election looked good. A Washington Post/ABC News poll found that 63 percent of the respondents expected Clinton to make significant progress on the economy, and a competing poll put Clinton's favorability rating at 71 percent. The week before the Inauguration, a USA Today/CNN/Gallup poll found that 70 percent were "somewhat or very confident" of Clinton's ability to handle international crises. National expectations were high that he could improve the economy, reform health care, and protect the environment. Datahead's own private polls showed the same thing. It was a time to gush about government, when all those supposed moderates decided to come out of the closet and admit it: "My name is Bill, and hell yes, I like government."

"So whaddaya think of those polls?" I asked Roadtrip, who was always good for some reality check, even on Datahead.

"Good luck. Polls, schmolls. Most of that's out of his control, anyway," he said. "He's getting a hell of a bounce just because he's new and wears cool sunglasses behind the wheel of his Mustang. And the rest is in the hands of one of the phoniest gangs to hit this town since the original Carter bunch."

"Don't forget Nixon."

"Nixon was a tough son of a bitch. He hired survivors and genuine tough guys. They might have been phonies to the public but they were authentic political assassins. You wanna do battle? Who would you want on your side? The Clinton crowd's going to shake their academic and policy credentials at you, give you a disapproving yuppie stare, invoke some psychobabbly schlock, and maybe send a memo with the White House seal to really scare you. The Nixon crowd would have rolled those credentials up and shoved them into you. Sideways. Twice, and the second time just for fun."

(In *Better than Sex*, Hunter S. Thompson wrote that Nixon's "political instincts were so dangerous that he made the politics of total opposition a very honorable trade for two generations of the best people in America. He gave no mercy and expected none. He was fun.")

Roadtrip had a point. According to a *Wall Street Journal* study, sixteen out of twenty cabinet-level appointees had law degrees or doctorates, and to a person they'd be hard-pressed to be able to explain what an oak leaf cluster was (you get it for serving your country in combat). A fifth had studied in England, and glaringly not in Viet Nam. Many had struck it rich in the 80s, something that clearly didn't matter to Clinton once elected. Making money in the 80s was sinful, but not if you were a Democrat. (The Whitewater-related revelations of Hillary's questionable $100,000 overnight commodities profits were known only to Bill and Hillary at this time and to a few former Arkansas stockbrokers now living on pigeons and garbage in Little Rock public parks.)

Hillary wasn't the only one in touch with the intellectual swamis. Clinton had his yogi too. David Osborne is the author of *Reinventing Government*, the book that had quickened the pulse of the big government crowd through its message that yes, after all, government could be made to work if only it was "reinvented"—reinvented, of course, by the smart set drawn from Clinton's *credentialistas.* Al Gore loved this concept. In time it became popular because in the midst of all the scandals and spin patrols, there was nothing left for the administration to hang onto.

Devotees formed an "Alliance for Reinventing Government" to spearhead this push. Along with Osborne, the alliance was headed by then-Oregon Governor Barbara Roberts, who in an interview told the *National Journal* on 3 April 1993 that "...actually government is leading change.... One of the things that Bill Clinton brings to my sense of hope about this kind of change is that he's been a governor for so long a time."

(Such sharp political instincts, by the way, contributed to Barbara's becoming by 1994 one of the most unpopular governors in Oregon history; she was bullied out of her reelection bid by street-smart former Democratic Oregon Senate President John Kitzhaber.)

Even after the nationwide repudiation in 1994, the Clinton administration could not give up its fascination with "reinventing" government. As late as 15 March 1995 White House press secretary Mike McCurry announced the "reinvention" of the foreign affairs apparatus. The next day the president himself went to a White House–organized reinventing government event in Arlington, Virginia. Clinton had brought along best-selling author Philip Howard as a political trophy wife. Howard, as it happens, is big in reinventing circles. *Wall Street Journal* reviewer Walter Olson described how "politicians of both parties have been falling over each other to declare that they are Howardites. Like him, they see that paperwork, litigation, and rulemaking have gone beyond all bounds of common sense."

The event was Clinton at his best:

> I think government can be as innovative as the best of our private sector business. I think government can discard volume after volume of rules.... We are about to get a bill out of the Congress which will

restrict the ability of Congress to impose mandates on state and local governments that are unfunded....

"Which Clinton and his White House domestic policy staff fought tooth and nail," a Republican Capitol Hill staffer told me with undisguised contempt. "And don't forget his other line from the speech—'Today we're announcing the first big step of what I assure you is just the beginning of a process that we intend to continue for as long as we have the public trust.'"

"'As long as we have the public trust'!" the staffer jeered. "What's this—March 1995? Did the November elections just not happen? Those people are living in a dream world."

"Well, sort of," sighed one of the few White House staffers vaguely in touch with current political reality. "The problem is not that making government more efficient is a bad thing. It's just that no one believes Clinton when he says it." The essence of Bill Clinton, the staffer explained, is an eternal search for a formula, for something that works as opposed to something he believes in. He cannot fall back on a set of core beliefs because he has none and is therefore compelled to undertake a search that will never reach its end.

(What is so striking is that the White House still found inconceivable that average citizens just might take things into their own hands and do some reinventing of their own, as they did in November 1994.)

Reinventing government was so trendy that the administration created its very own electronic "reinventing government" site on the Internet. The administration stacks trends on top of trends and pronounces it to be government. With a click of your computer mouse, you too could visit the reports of the "National Performance Review" and read about Vice President Al Gore's belief that "Government is starting to work better and cost less." According to Gore, "Over 90 percent of the National Performance Review's recommendations are under way with teams of government employees leading the way."

Better yet, if that doesn't jolt your juices, you can even get a "hypermedia version" (as if the media weren't hyped enough) as well as the "U.S. Government's first comprehensive set of published customer service standards." Which gives them, you realize, one more layer of bureaucracy with which to frustrate you completely. Fobbing the "first comprehensive set of public service standards" onto the public is like the West Coast's great white shark population issuing navigational charts to sea lions.

Roadtrip was not impressed.

"Putting customers first? I'll tell you about putting customers first. And they're right about that. You know what it takes do get an appointment or a meeting with Al 'Mr. Reinventing Government' Gore? A minimum of fifty grand in soft money to the DNC for the 1996 campaign. That's what I call a real good customer. You don't believe me? Call the son-of-a-bitch up yourself, and see if you can get in the front door with no money. I can see it now: you call Al, Al's not home, you call again, Al's still not home, you cut a check to the DNC, and all of a sudden you're leading the fast break for whoever you're pimping for to get the meeting and you pull up at the top of the key of life and let loose that fadeaway jump shot—"

"So what turned you into the Dick Vitale of the Clinton administration?" I asked.

"Because every day in this town is awesome, baby, AWESOME," Roadtrip practically shouted, "and it's twenty seconds to go in the Final Four, baby, thirty seconds left in the second half and you're down by one and your team's got the ball and you're on point, baby, and you got the rock in your hand and you're thinking NOTHIN' BUT NEEEET!!!" Roadtrip shrieked in his best Dick Vitale imitation.

He had a point. Washington is Powertown, the place where you gotta go to change the world, or to get a slice of the action where someone else is spending money to change the world. And it's wide, wide open. Washington is America's biggest crapshoot, bigger than Vegas, better than Powerball, more addicting than heroin. The only rules in this town are the ones you have the nerve to impose. Washington is the last frontier, a place where people reinvent themselves daily. People are drawn to Washington because it's the last place in America where you can always be more powerful than someone else. There are hundreds and hundreds and thousands of jobs, slots, and positions that have some sort of connection with the political culture. According to Washington representatives, the exhaustive yearly encyclopedia of the capital's lobbyists, over 15,000 are registered or have firms, and that doesn't count associates, researchers, and others who would multiply that figure fourfold. And somewhere, somehow, everyone can be a lord in their time. This is the great goal of the town, to be a lord to be listened to, to be considered important, if only in some small backwater operation on the fringe of the money and the smell of the rush when you put something into play somewhere, somehow, someplace. Washington is the Valhalla of *homo politicus*, the place to make your bones and run with the big dogs. It's the chance to play in a town of players, the game with the most extensive minor-league farm system in the world. It does not favor the youngest or the strongest, but the coldest and the toughest.

Roadtrip, who not only had the stomach but the survival skills, also had an even better assignment in these wild times. Roadtrip had no intention of joining the Clinton administration despite his vaguely Democratic leanings that grew remarkably more pronounced as George Bush headed toward a crash landing on the glide angle of a dropped set of keys. He possessed, however, a bloodhound's nose for the score.

Roadtrip, like most lobbyists, loved a winner. He had attended both the Democratic and Republican national conventions. In addition to schmoozing at cocktail parties and buying fancy dinners

for Bush administration officials and their counterparts in a potential Clinton campaign, Roadtrip made it a point to collect as many
convention buttons as possible. He doted equally on "Bush-
Quayle" and "Clinton-Gore."

"You wear their convention buttons on Election Day evening,
and you make a good symbolic impression," Roadtrip explained.
"See, you get wired with the big boys with money. Money's all that
talks in this town. You seed the campaigns like a wet ripe farm field.
Money makes it all grow. Money not only opens the doors, it creates the doors. My firm takes care of the money."

"So why waste your time with buttons?"

He looked at me gravely, as if I were missing something important. "Because there's always some pencil-necked campaign geek to
whom the whole thing is a holy crusade. He carries suitcases, gets
coffee, works twenty-eight hours a day, does anything. He projects
his persona, his soul onto the crusade of the campaign. These people are dangerous because they're worse than true believers.
They're obsessed, and they've made the campaign the central feature of their personal life story. Look at any campaign anywhere. If
you open your eyes you see them at the margins of the meetings,
on the circles of the crowd. But they all have one thing in common.
They watch. They listen, they look, they watch, they soak in anything and everything."

"O-kay…, " I said slowly. "What's that still get you?"

"Because all those campaign geeks have something else in common: more than one of them makes it to the top. See that sumbitch
over there sharpening pencils and running errands? Next thing you
know, one of them on the winner's side is going to be doing that at
the White House, at Treasury, at the Environmental Protection
Agency, at Commerce. I don't give a shit who pours coffee in general. I care a great deal about who pours coffee at the White House.
They can tell me who they're pouring coffee for, and when, and
where, and what time; who gets in the door, who's waiting, who

wants to but never will. And they know it from the git-go, those obsessed people at the bottom but on the inside, and they relish it immediately—it's the first time they actually have something to put into play with a name on it.

"You see it in the new congressional offices, too," Roadtrip continued. "Look at the operations of any of the freshman members, look real closely, and either in Washington or back in the district, you'll find that at least one of the staffers has made the jump from campaign flunky to congressional staff. And for them, it's wide-open from that point on. So that's why those things tell me volumes when the nut-cutting starts to happen. And that's something else about this business. The big boys always hire the coffee pourers. How do you think George Stephanopoulos got started?"

Roadtrip had known of Stephanopoulos from Capitol Hill. "George got his start in politics," he went on, "because there was no boot too low to kiss, no spittle too low to lick. That's another great secret of politics: the amount of ass-kissing you are capable of sanctifies your credentials and paves the path to power, not the other way around. You want brilliance? There's more brilliance than you could ever want in this country, Ph.D.s chock-full of brilliance, universities and think-tanks filled to the brim. What's really in short supply—and the George Stephanopouloses know this better than anyone else, and there's a premium paid for it—is having an immense capacity for abuse, for being treated like shit by some ego-swollen politician over and over and over again. I know someone who's a confidant of George but talks about him anyway because George talks to the president. You wouldn't believe the amount of shit Bill Clinton feeds him at high volume, day after day after day. Hell, I'd wear those Italian gigolo suits and a zippy haircut, too, if I had to put up with that kind of abuse, just to get my mind off it. George is a clever guy, don't get me wrong, but it wasn't his brilliance that got him so close to Clinton. It was his capacity for pain."

I remembered Roadtrip's assessment when the *National Journal* reported that "someone who watched Stephanopoulos during the campaign concluded that his talent was in saying hard things nicely to his elders."

"I don't hang with no losers and neither do they."

None of them does. Lyn Nofziger wrote in his memoirs that friendship and loyalty are rare enough because politics is "where winning always comes first." And no town loves a winner as much as Washington. There's a great scene at the end of the movie *Under Fire*, in which Nick Nolte and Joanna Cassidy star as journalists caught in the 1979 Nicaraguan civil war. Ed Harris plays a mercenary for the Somoza dictatorship, and throughout the movie he is a hardbitten mercenary who shoots Sandinista baseball stars and innocent civilians with equal abandon. At the end, however, Nick Nolte finds him in a Managua town square, wearing a tropical shirt while waving Sandinista flags and shouting, "Viva la Revolucíon!"

And that was Roadtrip, grinning just as broadly on Election Night at Clinton-Gore headquarters and shouting "Viva la Revolucíon" with the best of them. His preconvention "Clinton-Gore" button was displayed prominently on one lapel, and a hard-to-find, pre–New Hampshire primary button was on the other. He later confided that he had paid "some serious money" for the button. But he had been convinced of its authenticity. Besides, he added, the only thing that counted was that the Clinton crowd thought it was real, and they did.

CHAPTER THREE

DEAR DIARY

FORTUNATELY FOR THE country, *homo politicus* has a fatal flaw: extreme narcissism, and nothing illustrates this more than the propensity to keep a diary.

The Washington diary is the stuff of imagined and real intrigue. Most great Washington stories involve a diary. In his recent memoir, *Washington Post* editor Benjamin Bradlee, for example, recounts going to the house of his sister-in-law Mary Meyer, a lover of President John F. Kennedy. Meyer had just been murdered on the C&O Canal, and Bradlee was looking for her diary. But CIA counterintelligence chief James Angleton already had it. Disastrous diary keeping is a bipartisan habit. Richard Nixon's presidency crashed on the tapes, which might be considered a diary for somebody too busy to write. Bob Haldeman was a more committed diarist than his boss. Haldeman was the first

Washington figure to put his personal writings on CD-ROM, and his was the first modern White House diary to record meticulously and dispassionately the hour-by-hour exercise of raw power (not to mention the public service of deflating the reputation of Henry Kissinger). More recently, there is the diary kept by U.S. Senator Bob Packwood of his sexual and political conquests. It sealed his fate. Other diaries, too, have pushed Washington's pulse: minor Treasury official Josh Steiner was an anonymous toiler until his diary became an issue in the Whitewater investigation. In a distinctly Washington mode, Steiner insisted he'd lied in his diary.

In a few short leaks of fate, the Year of Health Reform suddenly became the Summer of the Diary. Delicious passages from Steiner's diaries tumbled one after another over Clinton's Washington. In this self-confessional day and age of Oprah, the Internet, and the first president to embrace the discourse of our psychotherapeutic age, the irony is tasty.

As Oscar Wilde wrote, "I never travel without my diary. One should always have something sensational to read on the train." Stein's diary may not have been as sensational as Oscar Wilde's but, in its way, it contained some gems. One was Boy George Stephanopoulos's memorable phrase: "This conversation never happened."

The Steiner diary, alas for the administration, indicated President Clinton and his staff had wanted to keep tight political control over the Whitewater investigation. Steiner wrote that George Stephanopoulos wanted to "find a way to get rid of" former U.S. Attorney Jay Stephens, who had been selected by the Resolution Trust Corporation to handle Whitewater.

The stock photo of Steiner reveals a brash, arrogant, almost smirking young man, one of the anointed "Stephanopouli," the network of administration aides who owed their jobs to George. With short, dark hair and blazing eyes, Josh could be George's clone.

When the inconvenient contents of Steiners's diary was made public, his lawyer, Reid Weingarten, subsequently told the press that it was "never Josh's intention that the diary would be a complete and accurate recordation of historical events." He described the diaries as "impressionistic efforts by Josh, written at some instances, weeks after events and for reasons that have nothing to do with the recordation of history."

Josh had been the fall guy. "[Acting White House Counsel Lloyd N.] Cutler got to him," Roadtrip guessed. "I heard they were up all night trying to find a legally defensible way to wriggle off that hook. And I heard there was tension between Cutler and Weingarten, too, over how much shit Josh was going to have to swallow to save George. See, Josh was being embarrassed, but George was looking at a potential obstruction of justice charge if they didn't play it right." Roadtrip, who never tired of mocking the way Stephanopoulos waved his "theological studies" around in the early days of the Clinton administration, when everyone was scrambling to prove their public spirituality, laughed and said, "God must have been on his side, or at least [Hillary's guru] Michael Lerner."

According to a White House source, both the president and the First Lady were "apoplectic" at the diarists. "President Clinton literally screamed at George [Stephanopoulos] at the top of his lungs," the source reported. "He was furious that they had kept diaries in the first place, and he was even madder that they had 'fessed up to them as well."

As a result of diarists, the public has had a window into the realities of Washington. The punditocracy had been convinced that exotica such as electronic town hall meetings would dominate public discourse. But instead it is the old-fashioned personal diary, the tool of choice for centuries to express human emotion and recorded history, that finds itself front and center today. History and society are better off as a result. Diaries are ultimately subversive. Diaries underscore the fundamentally human element of life in the political trenches: no numbers, no statistics, no theories, no absurdly complicated mathematical formulas, just real, raw emotion and plain, simple words—words with the power to change the way we think.

Such were Bob Packwood's diaries. One can only imagine his dismay when he learned that the Fifth Amendment did not protect his personal diaries. This ruling created a fair amount of fright in political circles. "Packwood is a victim," whined Mary McGrory, liberal *Washington Post* columnist. "Turning the investigation into an open-ended fishing expedition into his innermost thoughts is both unfair to Packwood and dangerous to us all," warned Nadine Strossen of the American Civil Liberties Union.

"Yeah," Roadtrip said when I showed him the Strossen quote. "We'd learn which of his staffers were better housekeepers than others, which ones did him with condoms and which ones didn't."

President Clinton wasn't the only one in the White House angry about the diaries. Hillary Rodham Clinton was snapping about the subject at anyone within sight or earshot for several days, and for more than one reason. You can only marvel at the possibilities contained in the mother lode of all Washington works-in-progress—the notes, musings, reflections, and intimate accounts that knowledgeable sources report were being compiled by none less than Hillary Rodham Clinton herself for a future book. "One of the first things she did was to seek an exact legal definition of what was and what wasn't a diary," a White House staffer told me. "She was terrified that her own papers might be discovered or subpoenaed as part of the congressional investigation. She's planning to write at least one, maybe two books about her years in the White House, and has been compiling materials and notes for it. She wanted to know if she had physically compiled documents in a file or a safe, would that be a diary or personal papers? Or what if she merely made a listing of documents and their locations—would that be a diary or would that be exempt? And when would it be a diary—when she actually and physically pulled them together? When she merely thought about doing it? She is crafty and is more interested in legal avoidances than broad concerns for doing the right thing. Things like that. I heard that once she referred to it as 'our presidency' in the company of several East Wing staffers, and then corrected herself immediately for the record. But they all felt like she had slipped and really meant it. She is worried about their place in history, but she's even more worried that Bill won't get it right—that whenever he writes his presidential memoirs, he'll concentrate too much on the policy details and not enough on broad historical vision."

The White House's reaction to the Whitewater investigation was not unusual. The political culture always shrieks in anger at outsiders who try to assert control over it. "You know what really freaked out the members in the House checking scandal?" said the legislative assistant to one of the Democratic members involved. "It wasn't the checks, the money, or the—excuse me while I guffaw—Ethics Committee. It was Malcolm Wilkey, the House Bank prosecutor who started sending letters of exoneration to members. The ones who got the letters in time were grateful. But the thought that their conduct could be judged by an outsider was just horrific. It was all they talked about. Wilkey, Wilkey, Wilkey."

Life on the edge of the political culture opens you to a world you never thought existed, a surreal, multidimensional place. On many occasions, throughout the 80s, I watched the fate and lives of people in faraway Nicaragua being bandied about by Democrats and Republicans like the breakfast on the table. It was just one more gathering of well-fed, middle-aged power junkies who wouldn't know a claymore from a cupcake.

Yet thousands of people willingly embrace the political culture year after year. And despite the endless potential of the diversity of background and experience, the people who participate in the political culture share the marks of the Fall of Politics.

First of all, they have their own language, as distinct and separate from the rest of America as everything else they have. When surgeon general nominee Henry Foster created a political firestorm in February 1995 over shifting accounts of how many abortions he had performed, the furor forced the White House to reexamine his background materials. On 21 February 1995, a reporter asked White House Press Secretary Mike McCurry, "Is this review of this FBI report, is this strictly a legal scrub or a political scrub?" not blinking, McCurry replied that the "scrub" was no big deal. No one asked any more questions about the "scrub."

Moreover, political people are consumed with, as a former Democratic Senate staff director put it bluntly, "Ego. Washington politics is ego. Large chunks of ego."

Another Democratic Capitol Hill staffer believes that politicians have a tremendous need for acceptance, almost a need to be loved. "When you look at the big ones like Clinton," he said, "you find the same things. The inability to say no. How they can find all kinds of ways to make you think they're on your side."

It can be especially difficult for newly elected Washington officials. "Suddenly, you're being surrounded by people totally dependent on you for their jobs and their life," the Senate staffer added. "It's the adoring staff syndrome. They hang on your every word while at the same time they are giving you, the politician, your words—they write them, they say them, they change them, they create them. That tends to isolate people from reality."

"And it gets worse," he continued. "There are people who want to be close to you because that is status—we're talking physically close. Do you meet the boss every day? Who knows that you do? Do you walk down the hall with him? People notice that. Do you chase him into the bathroom, briefing him as he enters the stall? It's a fast pace."

"On the other hand," the Senate staffer said with a smile, "don't forget the role of luck and timing, which creates the ability to be elevated spectacularly because of that proximity. Look at Carol Browner. She was an environmental legislative assistant for Al Gore when he was a senator, goes to Florida for two years, and bingo! She's the administrator of the U.S. Environmental Protection Agency. She wasn't even a committee staffer on Capitol Hill, for chrissakes. You think she'd be running EPA if she had been doing that LA [legislative assistant] work for [Sen.] John Kerry instead of Al Gore?"

They believe in clash and confrontation, the primacy of hostility, and the culture of the warrior. The speech of people in Washington is studded with the metaphor of gangs and prison mentality. Phil Keisling, *Washington Monthly* magazine editorial board member and Oregon secretary of state, commented on this phenomenon. "It's tribalism," Keisling said. "All this Bloods and Crips attitude about territory and respect leaves the country on the sidelines."

Keisling has a point, but I couldn't find many players who cared. "Nobody fucks with you, that's gotta be the word on the street," Roadtrip said. "I knew these two guys once in an office where they worked for a labor union. They had no conflicts, but one guy had his ear to the ground quicker than the other guy. So he leaks something to the newspapers that the other guy wrote privately, leaving no fingerprints of course, and made it look like the other guy did it by using his favorite expressions when he talked to the reporter, and just fucks the other guy cold, runs him out of the office, probably out of town for all I know. And you know why? He did it just to prove his bones. Just to show he could do it. No one fucked with him after that."

They are shameless. "Look at all the early photographs of the Clinton transition weeks after the election, and then into the early part of 1993," Roadtrip pointed out. "Who do you see everywhere? George Stephanopoulos. You would have thought that his main job during the transition was to get in all the pictures. He's next to Clinton's side, he's with Hillary, he's leaving Little Rock transition headquarters with Warren Christopher. And he did it on purpose.

"He told his friends that. He wanted to send the early message that he was the one with the juice, the access, the ear of the Man. Same with Mickey Kantor, except that he botched his first big power play to be White House chief of staff. Everyone thinks that George stuck it to him, and now it's part of George's legend. But I happen to know it was Clinton, who worked through George—George won the hand but took the heat, and Clinton got to use Mickey's considerable skills as Trade Rep, and then maybe something better after that."

It is a sea of podsnaps of Dickensian proportions—self-satisfaction and self-importance. A Democratic Capitol Hill staffer tells the story of young, Clinton-flushed White House staffers walking into an expensive Washington restaurant in 1994.

"We'd like a table," a group of them said firmly while the staffer was nearby.

"There are no tables available right now," the maître d' replied.

"We're from the White House."

"I'm sorry, there are no tables available."

"You don't understand. WE'RE FROM THE WHITE HOUSE."

CHAPTER FOUR

WHO ARE
THESE PEOPLE?

YOU, ON THE OTHER hand, have every right to ask where these people are from. Who are these political people, these insiders, the permanent government, the cultural elite who determine so much of the fate of our country in ways you will never be allowed to know?

I popped into town one fine day in May 1994 and found myself standing on the Metro station platform in Alexandria, Virginia, watching one limousine after another disgorge and pick up passengers at the Embassy Suites Hotel. The passengers looked well fed and even better dressed, expensive suits, genuine leather briefcases—the smell of affluence, even from this distance, was everywhere. My fellow passengers all clutched their morning bible, the *Washington Post*, the capital's premier political mood ring. They were the massive surge of white men in suits who make Washington the Mont Blanc pen capital of the world.

This is the stuff of the Fall of Politics, and that morning was just like any other morning in this time. Paula Corbin Jones's sexual harassment lawsuit against Bill Clinton had crashed onto the front pages that day. Ominously for Clinton, a lunar eclipse would take place at 1:27 P.M., an ill omen for rulers in primitive times because it was a sign of the passing of control from ruler to shaman.

And this is not a town short on shamans.

I walked into the subway car sporting my "I Still Believe in a Place Called Hope" Clinton badge. It produced wary looks. Wearing a Clinton badge on Election Day was one thing. Wearing it a year and a half later was insanity. Who would be that crazy? The men in suits and tan trenchcoats darted glances at me and then turned away.

They are the women and men of wealth and, within Washington's twisted standards, fame. They're not like the rest of us. Each one, in his or her own way, has embraced the political culture wholeheartedly. Each one, facing the moment of the Fall of Politics, surveyed the human and political landscape of the culture and decided that somehow, sometime, and in some advantageous way, some part of the fruits of that culture could be his or hers. At that private point, they left the rest of society behind and became *homo politicus*.

And they all love it, the conflict and girding up to test themselves and their skills on the lists of democracy. Author and Viet Nam veteran William Broyles has written about the secret love men have for war. Confronting a pile of enemy bodies loaded onto mechanical mules like so much garbage, Broyles "stood on the edge of [my humanity], looked into the pit, and loved what I saw there."

So it is with politics and *homo politicus*. And if politics is mortal combat by other means, Washington is a human strip mine. The disaster—from the Democratic point of view—of health care reform? The true pros express a perverse love for the edge of Broyles's pit. It is clutching, grasping, using, with any authentic humanity or emotion held hostage. A former Democratic Senate staffer put it bluntly, "You are who you work for. If the answer is Congressman Schmoe, the response is oh, that's nice, how nice for you. But if the answer is Dole, or Gingrich, or Clinton—well, that's different, people snap to attention. It's all derivative power—and it gets you laid, among other things."

Who you date depends on how you rate. Look at George Stephanopoulos. Who wanted to date a scrawny geek with an over-sized head who drenched himself in policy and politics twenty-four hours a day? Then all of a sudden he picks the right horse and he's in the White House. Calling all babes....

All is given to—and demanded by—the great game. One sus-pends commitments of family, relationships, a spiritual life. Sure, there's lots of talk, and this town is one big buzzword factory. But when ten-, twelve-, and fourteen-hour days are common—and cel-ebrated, worn on one's sleeve like a badge of honor and bragged about—where is the time, literally, for spouse and children? For friends? For church? A former Capitol Hill subcommittee staff director now living in the Southwest says firmly, "Washington is the opposite of life."

Homo politicus presupposes its values are the norm. Newspapers record regularly the shock expressed by the political culture at the reaction of the rest of the country when its practices are exposed. One of the most outrageous and infuriating examples was former Speaker of the House Thomas Foley, who in 1992 proclaimed that the members of Congress who abused the House bank by over-drafting thousands of checks were the "victims" of an angry public and media. (Most Americans took issue with Mr. Foley and pre-ferred the word "perpetrator.")

The dance of Washington is timeless, and the partners are always the same—legislators and lobbyists. In his classic work *The Lobbyists*,

Wall Street Journal reporter Jeffrey Birnbaum described a "micro-cosm of Washington: lawmakers and lobbyists moving together in a largely closed and isolated system, discussing decisions that affect millions of Americans.... [It] illustrated the earliest stage of what lobbyists do: gather information and develop contacts."

Washington being what it is, not everyone approves of the activities of Roadtrip and his tribe. Nader gadfly Joan Claybrook, for example, shaking her finger in *USA Today*, stated, "There are major distortions in our economy, and these affect the efficiency, the effectiveness, the fairness of the economy, and they're caused by subsidies and tax breaks, and loan guarantees, and insurance and other disbursements from the Treasury that are achieved by lobbyists that are looking out for their own clients and their own interests. And these come primarily through campaign contributions, rather than having a rational budget policy for the decision-making on our budget."

As Birnbaum observed, "Washington has become a club in which the line between those inside and those outside of government is not clearly drawn."

"Huh?" Roadtrip was mystified when I mentioned this to him. "Sure there's a line. We draw it, and we're always on the right side of it. What are we supposed to do? The political system isn't a license to talk. It's a license to hunt, and you get to eat what you kill. But that's not the whole story." He continued, "Sure, you want the bucks. But for most of us, I'll tell you another secret: we use the firm and the clients so we can play. You want to make real money? Go to Wall Street, mergers and acquisitions, divorce law. This town is for players."

And play they do. Washington's factional warfare had always taken place under the blood flag of no quarter. But since Democrats had been out of practice since 1976, the disorganization and chaos made the infighting and jockeying for position and influence after the 1992 election even more brutal than usual. One friend likened it to the Afghani sport of *buzkashi*, a combination of polo and foot-ball that uses a calf carcass and tears it to shreds by fighting for it on horseback over the steppes. "The less people understand how to do things, the more savage it becomes," he said. In this town, the calf carcasses have names and families.

Roadtrip would be navigating in unsettled seas at best, and as my guide, he agreed to let me follow his progress to a degree. It was more than useful. I had spent nearly all of my Washington experi-ence in the House of Representatives. I knew the Hill, but the rest of that vast world beyond—the lobbyists, clients, consultants, how the regulatory agencies played—was beyond my personal experience.

"So I'm not gonna be your headlight, and don't forget it," he told me at the outset.

"You mean *in* the headlight."

"I mean either place. That would be it. I mean, look. I'm no Clark Clifford or Tommy Boggs. I don't make rain fall out of the sky. A little mist and drizzle every now and then, okay. There's fif-teen thousand people like me in this town. I have to work for my action. I go public, I'd be buns up in a town that can't tell mating season from a hog slaughter. You understand?"

I understood. One of Roadtrip's more pleasant qualities is his tendency to lapse into Southern-fried, cornpone platitudes when he needed to make an important point, and that one was typical. The smell of Clinton's Arkansas was in the air, and he was sniffing. During the early Bush administration, right after the victory over Michael Dukakis, he'd spent a fair amount of time reading up on Down East and pouring through L.L. Bean catalogs, only to dis-cover that the Bush crowd talked more Texan than chowder. "Learning Texas was easier than Maine because they talk a lot more," he observed. "And it's easier to sound like a Texan. All you have to do is pretend you've had a prefrontal lobotomy, chase a shot of tequila with a glass of ammonia, and you'll be good old-boying with the best of 'em in a New York minute."

A "New York minute," Roadtrip discovered, is a classical Texas phrase that encodes the Texan's sense that New Yorkers move quicker and faster than real life. In reality, of course, New Yorkers move at normal modern speed but seem fast by comparison, especially in the critical area of linear thought process.

"Take the House banking scandal a couple of years ago, where hundreds of members of Congress were writing checks with no money to back them up." I knew it well; my former boss, U.S. Rep. Ronald Coleman (D-Tex.), had overdrafted 676 checks for nearly $300,000 in a scandal that had nearly cost him his congressional seat.

"But it wasn't a secret, was it—not to insiders. Everybody knew you could float paper at the House bank and not have it bounce. Staffers did by the thousands, and you know who else? The goddamn press, specifically the Capitol Hill press corps. They could write checks at the House bank, too, and I happen to know they floated their share. Everyone in the Hill community knew about it—everybody except the public, which was understandably outraged when the story finally broke."

One of Roadtrip's most endearing qualities is his ability to know the difference between what he tells his clients and what he believes himself. This is not always the case among lobbyists. After all, you have to have a certain amount of civic pathology within you to do the job in the first place. But to a client, a lobbyist is more than an attorney or a writer of bill language. He or she serves as part shaman, part priest, bridging the chasm between supplicant and the great mystery called Washington. The lobbyist performs the rituals, makes the entreaties, and tries not only to predict the future, but also to bend it to the will of the client. There's a lot of handholding and babysitting in the process, too, but at most lobbyists' hourly rate, it's worth the hassle.

Roadtrip, on the other hand, knew that the truth was both simpler and more complicated at the same time. Most of the business is cash and carry, and has less to do with the eloquence of your testimony before a regulatory agency or how many parties you throw, and more to do with how much money you have available to spread around. He can play the role of the veteran Washington hand with the best of them, but in private he is refreshingly candid.

"My problem with so many people in this town is that they start believing their own rap and then their own rep," he said. "It's one thing to solemnly defend your right to petition the legislature, to pontificate about the need for every point of view to be heard in order to make the democratic process work. It's another thing entirely to actually believe that crap. And *I* don't. Look who's getting hired. You take your basic dumb-ass representative like [Minnesota] Rep. Gerry Sikorski, who lost his seat in the wake of the House checking scandal and should have lost it several years ago when former aides talked to the press about Gerry's wife making them take her dogs to be artificially inseminated. Does he crawl back to the land of the ice and snow whence his people came? Hell, no. He gets hired to head the Washington office of a Minneapolis law firm doing the same issues for paying customers that he did while a member. You think the law firm cares how many checks he floated? Please."

Roadtrip was candid about those who play the Washington games, both lobbyists and politicians. He was not the only one who had learned to give good Arkansas. In mid-November 1992, Frank Mankiewicz of the lobbying firm Hill and Knowlton threw a party that featured fried green tomatoes, curried okra, and catfish. Mankiewicz's authenticity was questioned, however, when *Newsweek* magazine reported that the meal was not real Arkansas. A spurned caterer sneered that real Arkansas cuisine is pure "garbage" and includes Twinkie pies.

"Frank is at his best on all fours," Roadtrip muttered, adding, "and from what I hear about those dark Ozark hollows, you should consider yourself lucky if everything they serve you is simply dead."

There was plenty of political roadkill during the Democratic presidential transition, and Hillary was usually the one behind the wheel with her high beams on. "It's an ugly game at the top, especially with Hillary and her *tanda* carving up Democratic careers wholesale, left and right," Roadtrip reported. It was a good choice of terms—*tanda* refers to one's particular graduating class in Central and South American military dictatorships, and one's loyalty is always to the *tanda* first, not your country or even the military as a whole—and from what I heard from other sources, entirely accurate.

"Look," Roadtrip would point out a year later, "Bill and Hillary were still climbing in that heady spring of 1993 when all things looked possible. It wasn't enough to win the presidency; they were going to own you spiritually as well."

Other presidents' wives could be tough, of course. Of Nancy Reagan, Lyn Nofziger said, "If you screwed up and in the process embarrassed her husband, or hurt him politically, or in any other way, or if she thought that you had, she got mad—at you.... When you got on Nancy's special list, life could become somewhat less pleasant."

Being on the enemies list of a traditional president's wife is one thing. But the advent of Hillary has brought about two separate and often equal loci of presidential power instead of one. As a result, her personality can distort the policymaking process, especially inside the White House. This dagger-like vindictiveness extends toward people on their own side, and sometimes even more so. A Democratic Capitol Hill staffer who served on the White House's massive and secretive 1993 health care reform task force was still bitter a year later: "With Hillary, the one thing you do not want to do is be the one to raise anything objectionable, or facts, data, comments that prove her wrong. That cannot and must not be done."

He shook his head as if he still could not believe what a disaster she had brought for his party and for an issue in which he happened to believe deeply and personally.

"If you do raise objections or bring up facts contrary to her beliefs, guess what happens?" he asked. "You don't get invited to the next meeting. You're out of the loop. That's what happened to [David] Gergen." Another staffer on the same task force reported the same thing: "She smiles but she looks at you like you're a menu."

Okay now, dear reader, hold on. Let's stop for a minute and get a couple of things straight. All of these people in Washington, from Bill and Hillary to the lowliest legislative correspondent on Capitol Hill—you need to understand two essential things about Washington: one, *these are not normal people*, and two, *there are no normal people there*.

Washington politics is run by *homo politicus*, not normal people, and it's a fundamental lesson to remember. Cult film freaks: remember the test that Harrison Ford administers to the android "replicants" in the movie *Blade Runner*? He measures changes in the eye's pupil reaction to determine whether someone is a human being or a replicant. Sometimes it took thirty or forty questions to make an educated guess, but here's a sure-fire way to tell the difference between *homo politicus* and normal people without leaving home.

The only equipment you need is a television with a remote control zapper.

First, use your remote to turn your television to the C-SPAN channel. Now punch in the direct channel number to MTV (okay, VH-1 if you're over forty). If your zapper is like most, it has a jump button that allows you to switch back and forth instantly between those two channels.

Glance at your watch. Sit back, pop a beer, and enjoy your favorite music videos for seven minutes exactly. Now go back to C-SPAN.

Chances are you're going to catch some anal-retentive, beef-fed Republican in full stride and florid of face, carping about something he wished had happened back in the good old '80s. Or perhaps a sniveling, blow-dried Democrat whining about the plight of poor people with all the sincerity of a 1-900-number psychic.

You start feeling weird, uneasy. Zap back to MTV. Hang around for a minute or two.

Now zap!

"Mr. Speaker, I rise in support of the motion to amend the joint resolution…"

The hair on the back of your neck starts to curl. You begin to wonder if your wife ate the last of the Tums.

Relax again with music videos for one minute exactly. Here comes the tough part again…

Now zap!

Got you another three-piece-suited sucker, no doubt.

As your throat begins to constrict involuntarily, take the zapper out of your hand and place it on the couch. Stare intently and PAY ATTENTION to the man or woman talking on the House floor. Do not, under any circumstances, look at the zapper.

Check your watch. How long until your hand begins to quiver?

How long until you suddenly shriek without warning and start bashing the buttons on your remote in an uncontrollable, drooling frenzy to do whatever it takes RIGHT NOW to get that sneering politician's snout off your television's screen?

The national record for normal people watching C-SPAN is just under seventeen seconds. (It's held by a woman professionally trained in negative-ion visualization avoidance theory.)

Congratulations. Despite your pain, you have successfully passed the test. You are, from the standpoint of politics, a normal person.

Now here's the shocking part: *the* homo politicus *doesn't react that way at all!*

To a person, the *homo politicus* cannot engage the brain to execute that first zap back to MTV. And that says it all: these are not normal people. Corollary: there are no normal people here.

CHAPTER FIVE

BILL CLINTON
AND THE FALL OF POLITICS

*The President said that [former First Lady Jacqueline Kennedy Onassis]
inspired him and an entire generation of Americans to see the nobility of helping others and the good that could come in public service.*
> —White House statement, 20 May 1994, on remarks
> by the president at UCLA's seventy-fifth anniversary

WHITEWATER, HILLARY, *the federal government shutdown,
the budget crisis, the national paralysis—so we have Kennedy to blame
for all this?*

Snapshot: Spring 1996.

It's right after high noon in the highest-ever budget battle
stakes between President Bill Clinton and Republican leaders in
Congress. Americans are still getting over having watched in
amazement as a parade of follies and foibles unfolded in front of
them:

Finger-pointing from every direction and by all sides, and not all
of it done with the index finger;

The entire crisis has become a theater of the absurd in the wake of
House Speaker Newt Gingrich's remark that the reason he had put
such tough provisions in the budget was that he hadn't been shown

61

enough respect by the president on an Air Force One flight to the funeral of slain Israeli Prime Minister Yitzhak Rabin.

Long-winded media explanations of why a difference of nine one-hundredths of 1 percent between the president and Congress could lead to the six-day shutdown.

And, if all that wasn't enough, the astonishing sight of the first First Lady in U.S. history to be hauled before a federal grand jury probing allegations of financial fraud and other criminal acts that stem from the First Lady's wheeling and dealing in the savings and loan industry when her husband was still governor of Arkansas.

As polls showed the public increasingly blaming the whole lot of them, Democrats and Republicans alike, no one asked the big question: Why would anyone trust White House or congressional economic projections in the first place? Neither one has ever been on the money from the early '80s on.

To many Americans, the budget impasse showed that the collective national political culture was crazy, pure and simple.

Who are these people, these politicals who control so much of the fate of the nation yet combine it with so little regard for the future of the country?

Or better yet, *what* are they?

Snapshot time again: Fall 1992.

Amidst the hosannahs of adoring columnists, Bill and Hillary Rodham Clinton win the presidency in a landslide. "First Baby Boom President Faces Huge Tasks," the *Washington Post* screams in a headline. The *Post* anoints the boy president the "self-styled heir to a legend." "After 12 Years of Republican Rule, a New Era Emerges" is the general tenor of the media projections.

It is a great day for the in-crowd. *The War Room* becomes a cult flick, and child wizard George Stephanopoulos gets to date celebrities. A new age of good feelings about government, Democrats, and life in general dawns in a capital basking in the glow of Democratic hegemony of the White House, the Senate, and the House of Representatives. Draped in white, Hillary Clinton in May adorns the cover of the *New York Times Magazine*. Headline: "Saint Hillary." In the piece, the First Lady announces to America's graying New Age Children the advent of the "politics of virtue." The crowing has started in earnest. *Washington Post* reporter Martha Sherill leads the cheers:

> He sings "Love Me Tender." He drives an old convertible. He and Hillary—who named their daughter after a Joni Mitchell song—like to hang around the kitchen at night, sitting on the counters, eating takeout and gabbing about policy with all their propeller-head friends. With Clinton as president—will he be inauguarated as "Bill?"—we'll see more Hollywood trend-o-morphs at state dinners, hear more bad '70s rock music, feel more envy. *He's only 44, for God's sake.*
>
> A generational—and social—shift is obviously upon us. The whole moneyed, starchy, dignified, anti-intellectual, Ivy League, blue-blazered, country club, comatose, conservative culture is passing before our eyes—and retiring. But liberal baby boomers must remember not to be mean or to gloat. After all, everybody deserves a proper burial.
>
> Liberal apologist Michael Kinsley wrote simply, "Allow me to gloat."

Snapshot again: Summer 1994.

Reality has set in. Others gloat now, and Mr. Kinsley has been reduced to a whine: the Clintons are on the ropes, health care reform (once the playpen of Hillary and Ira Magaziner) is dead, and Democrats are not only running from the president in the midterm elections but from their own party label. The nation is up in arms about the Clintons's lying, Whitewater, and other scandals. We sense a general lawyering of the truth. The deepest cut of all is the revelation that, just like the Republican Wall Streeters of the '80s she professed to abhor, Saint Hillary made a sweet $100,000 killing in the cattle futures market via a partnership with a gang of Arkansas good old boys. The polls barely detect a political pulse. The largest crowd roar at the annual rodeo in Polson, Montana, is for a 400-pound pig named "Swillary." Agriculture Secretary Mike Espy is on the way out on corruption charges, and HUD Secretary Henry Cisneros is in hot water for paying hush money to his mistress and lying about it to the FBI. Eighties' bagman Tony Coelho is fronting for the DNC. The history of the administration is a string of mantra-like phrases signifying scandal: "Zoe Baird-nannygate-Whitewater-Paula Jones-Vince Foster-Hillary's commodity killings-Ron Brown-Mike Espy-blah-blah-blah."

After a year and a half, reports that Clinton might possess backbone are about as reliable as UFO sightings.

A Fellini-like atmosphere reigned in Washington; acting as if the last two years had simply not happened, Vice President Al Gore announced with breathtaking chutzpah on 10 June 1994 that "cynicism" drains us of the will to improve; it diminishes our public spirit… it withers our souls."

Cynicism?, you might ask with a straight face. You mean we had anything to do with public cynicism? From an administration that instructed its officials not to describe the mass killings of Tutsis by Hutus in the Rwandan holocaust as "genocide"?

Three weeks later, Gore pronounced the "reinventing government" effort to be a success.

Another snapshot: Late 1994.

And what a success it was, except that the voters did the real reinventing of government. Bill Clinton did indeed change the way Washington does business: his failed policies and leadership led to the historic Republican triumph of 1994. The Augean stables had been flushed out by the Republican tidal wave of 1994. Hillary and her sneering preachiness have become all but invisible; you can find her only on White House Christmas cards and subpoenas.

Hunter S. Thompson produced the quote of the year: "Hillary Clinton has the voice of a raven born from a black egg."

By early 1995, White House handlers had squelched the screech. Hillary might be doing recipes again and admiring rugs in the White House for *Parade* magazine, but the grown-ups weren't about to let her near policy or Congress again. The decision was the result of internal White House discussions termed "extremely strained" by a firsthand source, with Mrs. Clinton continuing to push to the end for a prominent role that would identify her with policy and showcase her as a leader. According to a White House source, a memorandum written by another aide (a copy of which the source found in a photocopy machine) for a personal diary laid out Hillary's newer, "softer" role, which included a series of media appearances beginning in early 1995 and calculated to reestablish her in the First Lady's traditional "women's issues" role—public declarations of admiration for Eleanor Roosevelt, for example, or pushing to improve the lives of the world's women at a UN conference in Beijing.

The memorandum also described the discussions as a difficult process, with the First Lady unwilling to concede a single mistake on her part. The White House inner circle was divided, with outside adviser Paul Begala reportedly as a leading advocate of "traditionalizing" Hillary.

"The smartest thing Bill Clinton did since winning the election was putting her on the road," a West Wing staffer told me in March 1995. "Look at all the commotion going on in Washington right now—the Contract with America, enormous budget cuts, even another round of Republican tax cuts so the GOP nominee in 1996 can run on them—can you imagine what a lightning rod she would be—especially if the president actually had the nerve to put her in charge of something again? So instead, he sends her to the Third World, home of banished vice presidents and ambassadorships to principalities and thugocracies handed out to campaign contributors."

"Besides," the same source snickered, "let me read you the official statement. 'First Lady Hillary Rodham Clinton'—known affectionately in our shop as Her Rodham Clintonness—

will make an official visit to five countries in South Asia March 24 to April 6. Her visit to Pakistan, India, Bangladesh, Nepal, and Sri Lanka is part of the Administration's continuing efforts to develop and strengthen U.S. relationships in this part of the world. In each country, Mrs. Clinton will meet with women representatives of government and nongovernment organizations, religious institutions, education, business and the arts. The First Lady will also visit communities to see firsthand how men and women are creating a 'seamless' Web of services as well as training, educational, and economic opportunities which support, empower, and nurture children and their families.

"Support, empower, nurture," I remarked. "I like the sound of it. Besides, her speech in New Delhi urged a stronger voice for women, that they should end their 'silence.'"

"Would that *she* were silent," the staffer sighed. ["I am woman. Hear me roar."]

The source would not let me see the memorandum or read from it directly for fear of exposure, but only described the contents in terms general enough to avoid detection, and even then from a pay phone. "There's fear that this place is so paranoid about leaks that they're making subtle changes in copies of memos so when they get leaked, they can be traced back to the original distribution list," the source explained. "[Bruce] Lindsey and others are dropping all kinds of hints about threats and retaliation for leaking." The president's media and political advisers were in on the debate, the source added, and claimed that Hillary's intransigence and initial refusal to change course meant that the president himself had to step in and make the final decision.

"Maybe, maybe not," Roadtrip said darkly when I told him about the memorandum.

"Maybe not what?"

"She's sharp, and she knows how to cut her losses," he replied. "Maybe the debate was a sham. Maybe the debate never happened. Maybe they're planting stories like this to create confusion, in which case the press will just accept the new and improved Hillary at face value. That Begala's a slick bastard, you know. Maybe you weren't supposed to be the one who heard about it. Maybe that was a screw-up. Maybe it's because someone like Stephanopoulos got her sent to Africa while a lot of 1996 campaign decisions were being made in the White House—or maybe it's a rival of Begala who wants her to *think* he's out to get her."

"You're as crazy as those hamsters in the White House," I remarked.

"That's a way of life in Camelot," he said. (And for whatever reason, Begala would be pushed out of the White House by mid-1995 and return to his native Texas.)

"So whatever did happen to the new Camelot?" I asked.

"I take clients there once a month," Roadtrip cracked. As male lobbyists know, Camelot is an upscale strip joint on K Street.

How did we go so fast from Democratic triumph to Republican takeover? It only took two years. The crushing collapse of the Clinton dream in so short a time is in many ways an exercise in expectations. But it also reveals something deep about the political culture itself. More is at work here than the general tawdriness of the Clinton administration (which is not uninteresting, don't get me wrong) or the institutionalized corruption in Congress.

It is something that goes to the very soul of Washington's political culture.

From the practiced unction of media commentators such as the American Enterprise Institute's Norman Ornstein, to the fallen barons of the political order such as defeated Speaker of the House Thomas Foley or First Lady Hillary Rodham Clinton—

or to the now-triumphant Newt Gingrich and the new crowd—
few challenge the single, overriding dogma of the political culture: that politics, and individual participation therein, is a
necessary and salvationary experience for both society and the
individual who engages in the practice of politics. Though Bill
Clinton and Newt Gingrich pursue radically different political
goals and have diametrically opposite views of what constitutes a
better nation, they share a common foundational view: that politics is the means by which they will transform America. They
not only believe they can practice politics without tainting themselves morally, but they will also, in fact, experience a personal
moral elevation as a result of their participation in politics.

"That would be news to Clinton's girlfriends and Newt's first
wife," Roadtrip noted.

Roadtrip has a point. Politics may transform society, but it does
not ennoble those who practice it. The underlying assumption of
Washington's *homo politicus* is that only those in political life can
properly lead society to recognize its faults and flaws, and then correct them through the political experience—as defined, of course,
by the professional political culture.

Nowhere was this made more clear than by Al Gore, in his Harvard Commencement Day Speech on 9 June 1994, when he
squarely placed the blame on society for America's current problems and prescribed politics as the cure. The salvation of the
nation, in his view, could never come from the country or its people, but only from the political process.

From Gore's assumptions, it follows that politics needs a priesthood: pundits. How often have we heard a graven-faced pundit
from the media or academia tell us on a Sunday talk show that
Washington is "complex"—and hence beyond the grasp of ordinary mortals?

Washington *can* be complicated. But there's a difference
between complicated and complex. How *do* you make sense out of

Washington? That's a good question. The blizzard emanating from the capital tells you nothing fundamental. But there is plenty of paper. The higher you go, the more paper you produce. *New York Times'* Maureen Dowd calls it "the permanent noise." Dowd added: "Even in a town built on blather, in a city that invented the filibuster, President Clinton and Newt Gingrich stand out for... the sheer, staggering, endless torrent of words they produce." If New York is the town that never sleeps, Washington is the town that never shuts up.

What all this means is that today's Washington goes far beyond the traditional committee hearing room or press conference. It rages on the airwaves and on the Internet, in millions of private conversations from the Oval Office to the town's massage parlors.

As a result, you will never know everything that goes on in Washington.

You will never know everything important that goes on in Washington.

You will definitely never know everything that's even marginally important in Washington.

You *can* know, however, the key operating element that pushes the dark force through the power: the Fall of Politics.

Here's how it works:

Washington might be complicated, but it is not complex. It's neither politics nor policy. Washington is, above all, people driven by the fundamentals of human existence. For all its vastness, for all the paper, the separation of the individual practitioner from others and the political culture from the rest of society means that it is still fair to ask the question: "What does Washington have to do with America?"

The first step is to forget the grinning political scientists on public broadcasting with their numbers and equations. Here's all the political theory you'll ever need:

Politics and government—on a fundamental level, the two are

entirely synonymous—do not offer a salvational experience despite the pleas of its devotees and their many references to history. Modern democratic theory and practice were born against the context of the theocratic state and absolute monarchy, and wrapped in Enlightenment thought. They inspired the American Revolution, the French Revolution, and the European democracies. The common thread was that public institutions were seen as a bulwark against private gain and greed. Today, however, the situation is reversed—private institutions and initiatives are the bulwark against government. Greed, once the vice of kings and aristocrats, is the most salient feature of government today.

"Democracy," as Roadtrip said, "is just one more thing we humans have fucked up."

(You want real theory? Go read real theory. Write when you find work. This is true theory. This is real life. Trust me. You'll see.)

No single individual today symbolizes this chasm between packaging and reality better than Bill Clinton. Trapped between the rhetoric of salvation and the politics of business as usual, he is being dragged down because the public is disgusted by the gulf between who he says he is and who he is. In 1993, Clinton pleaded for public support for his economic plan by attacking the political culture: "...the special interests will be out in force. Those who profited from the status quo will oppose the changes we seek.... Every step of the way they'll oppose it. Many have already lined the corridors of power with high-priced lobbyists. They are the defenders of decline.... "

Roadtrip, my favorite defender of decline, had been slouched in the shadows of the Capitol during Clinton's speech.

"You think anything's changing?" he scoffed. "I resent that. Clinton and his crowd just shook down the unions, corporations, and the deep-pocket crowd for $20 million in 'soft' money. Soft money goes into party-building activities like get-out-the-vote. Well, it's been a great party. Clinton won, and we paid for it because he asked us for it. Who does he think he is, anyway? Sooner or later that slip pery son of a bitch is going to learn he can't have it both ways. Change? Clinton's going to put a front man for Libya in charge at the Energy Department. Bob Packwood is the Senate's latest oral surgeon. It turns out that J. Edgar Hoover pranced around in pantyhose and negligees. You want Washington? That's Washington. That's change. I need a drink, and I'm late for a meeting."

Washington is a town of euphoric highs and manic lows. The collective mood hit rock bottom in early 1992 amid national uproar over the congressional check-kiting scandal, the perks, and the rest of Washingtonalia. In a matter of months, however, the mood was miraculously and dramatically transformed: Bill Clinton was elected president—the person who sets the taste of the town—and he was unabashedly a government man. Not only had he campaigned and won on a platform of decidedly activist government, he had won a platform of activist government in Washington.

It was money in the bank for the political culture.

The sharks were elated. "If things ain't moving, we're not moving," one lobbyist explained. "And if we're not moving, we're not making any money."

The smell of money and influence continued to waft gently over the Potomac from the very start of the Clinton administration. According to the Center for Responsive Politics, the average Senate winner in 1992 raised $1,047,042 from political action committees. The House was no different. "Both Democrats and Republicans in the House rely on PACs for a major portion of their overall revenues," the Center's Larry Makinson said, "but Democrats rely on PACs much more than Republicans [because of] the influence of labor union PACs, which gave over $40 million to Democrats in the 1992 elections and only $2.4 million to Republicans."

The late Democrat superlobbyist-turned-Commerce Secretary Ron Brown, who had apparently developed a personal economic plan of his own, was forced to cancel an inaugural gala in his honor thrown by corporations doing business with the Commerce Department. To make matters worse, Brown refused to say how he would handle contacts with his son, who worked for a lobbying firm representing Japanese interests and who is taking over many of his father's clients. Brown himself had represented a consortium of Japanese electronics companies against the interests of American workers in the 1988 trade bill. Haitian dictator "Baby Doc" Duvalier had also enlisted Brown's services. But Brown sailed through confirmation hearings, even though he flatly stated that he would abstain from dealing with matters involving his law firm for the first year only.

And that was just the beginning.

It didn't stop there. Much more was to come—Hillary's commodities, Whitewater, Hillary's explanations, Webb Hubbell, George Stephanopoulos's sweetheart deal on a house loan, and on and on and on. When you take the pious pronouncements of Bill's language of redemption, Saint Hillary's politics of meaning designed to stake a claim to a higher moral ground, the incessant references to George Stephanopoulos's theological studies—it all adds up to nothing more than a sleek package of slick New Age spirituality shtick, a political infomercial and about as authentic.

We'll see. In the meantime, something as old as human nature is at work: the Fall of Politics.

What is the Fall of Politics?

Simply put, it is the separation that occurs between an individual who has embraced the political life and the rest of society. It is also the gulf between society as a whole and the political culture.

Here's a story that made the rounds in Washington that shows how the Fall of Politics (as embodied in one ambitious yuppie couple) has affected the course of history:

It was February 1992, the peak of the New Hampshire Democratic primary, and Gennifer Flowers went public with her affair with Bill Clinton. Clinton learned, to his dismay, that the problem with the feminist assertion that "the personal is the political" has an inevitable reverse effect: the political is also personal. Thus panic ensued in the Clinton camp. Clinton had clearly had an affair with Flowers, campaign aides realized. They feared the end was near.

According to the story, Hillary Rodham Clinton got on a private call with Lloyd Cutler, the attorney and superlobbyist.

What am I going to do? she pleaded.

You have two choices, responded Cutler. You can go with your emotions and take this thing down, and ruin the chances for another generation of Democrats. Or you can swallow the pain and the humiliation, and go out in front of the cameras and stand by your man.

Pause.

Hillary finally replied. She posed the ultimate Washington question:

"What should I ask for?"

So much for change.

CHAPTER SIX

"YOU COULD BE MINE!"

THE MOST CONVINCING explanation of the Fall of Politics comes from Rousseau. Yeah—surprise—Jean-Jacques himself.

I wouldn't waste much time on the substance of his theories, but his intellectual architecture is brilliant. In the *Discourse on the Origins of Inequality*, Rousseau rewrote Genesis to construct the secular Fall of "natural man" into "civilized man." In essence, he argued that private property is the source of this corruption. The climactic moment came when natural man looked at something and said (in a phrase Rousseau made famous), "This is mine."

The philosopher's thoughts on private property might need a little work, but when it comes to American politics, both Genesis and Rousseau are right on the money. Here's why:

"Something happens."

How many times do you hear that phrase used by even hard-core political operatives to describe, in fleeting unguarded moments, the change that takes place within an individual as she or he progresses from one level of political practice to a more powerful one, and particularly after that momentous leap from the regional to the national?

Something happens, and you people might not believe what I have seen with my own eyes: that somehow, sometime, each in his or her own dark corner and in his or her own dark way, a fundamental transformation takes place, one in which the newly mutated *homo politicus* looks you in the eye and says, "You could be mine."

Not mere private property, but power and influence and the bargain with the dark side that it takes to get it. That is the moment of betrayal, the point at which somebody takes the ferry to the other side of the river and stays there. To embrace Washington's political culture is to engage in a blood purge of what you've left behind.

It's a moment that changes the soul.

A friend from the northwest asked me in 1993 what I had thought about President Clinton's timber summit. He expected a reply about the plight of the timber workers or the need to preserve ecosystems. Instead, I answered, "The east slopes of the Cascades are exempted to buy off House Speaker Tom Foley. The odds are that Clinton's going to split workers from management with a log export ban. The unions don't care where the trees come from, only that mills stay open. Plus, timber industry officials gave heavily to Bush, and the Clinton crowd has a long and mean memory. Maybe he'll throw in a little old growth to get the mills jump-started, a little retraining smoke and mirrors, but in the end it'll be one big kiss-off."

"How cynical can you get?" my friend snapped.

Our eyes met and I fell into the political equivalent of the thousand-yard stare.

"It can't be all that bad...."

I returned in an instant to a culture of countless deals and betrayals witnessed, a manipulation so deep and so ugly it often defied description, a daily life of shoot and cover, move and countermove, thinking three, four, ten moves down the road as any flickering of ideals or civic virtue was hunted down and gutted, person by person and soul by soul, ground viciously into the infected dust of some dark political alley and crushed out of existence. I thought of those who crashed and burned along the way, victims of bad luck, success, treachery, or some combination of the three. I tasted again the ambition and a will to power so strong that success breeds addiction and failure leaves a vengeful spirit. I thought of the lies, the lies to yourself and to others, lies for breakfast and lies with your scotch and jokes, lies so stupid and lies so blatant and hideous you bury the memories deep and fill the hole with a heavy black stone.

The moment passed, the fires flickered out, and I was still looking at my friend. "Let's hope not," I said, and left it at that. Would he have understood if I had told him the whole truth? I realized then I knew something he didn't. It wasn't truth as we normally think of it, but a secret window or hidden door to something that bordered on the unholy.

The key to understanding Washington beneath the surface lies in our *homo politicus*, a species of pure appetite produced by the Fall of Politics and capable of shedding more skins than a copperhead. *Homo politicus* is the one with the hungry gleam in the eye that says, "You could be mine."

Forget idealism, principle, justice, and the rest of the intangibles. To Washington insiders, the play's the thing. The official job description is irrelevant. As the great waves of national issues crash overhead, the teeming masses of *homo politicus* underneath are alternatingly fearful and smirking as they contemplate such matters as Clinton's forgotten middle-class tax cut or the clash over health care reform.

"The word 'reform' ought to be banned from our vocabulary," Roadtrip said. "When someone in this town talks reform, the smart money knows that someone else is going to take a gutting."

This, then, is the Fall, for those who have accepted the politician's bargain—the Fall of Politics and the fall of *homo politicus* himself.

Those who are quick enough and lucky enough to make it to the top rarely leave Washington. The allure of power is too great; the almost animalistic urge to keep one's hand in the game is too strong. Ask almost anyone in the business why he or she persists, and he will flash you that same crazed, off-center grin you see at Atlantic City blackjack tables at five o'clock in the morning. Political power is the real crack cocaine of Washington.

Many of those within the political culture will admit to some degree of awareness not only of this isolation, but of a sense that the culture might be under siege. But the moment does not last. You cannot push them farther. Each participant carries a personal black hole, the line beyond which he or she will not engage in self-examination.

Washington is less a town of respectable institutions than a conversation of thieves, a teeming casbah of hucksters, hustlers, scam artists, minor despots, and peacocks. And at its core, the real talk is not of issues or policy but of the scheming of those who will influence and decide the issues—who they will be, who they will not be, who will win, who will lose, and what the price will be. It is a collective conversation of perhaps fifteen to twenty thousand, all scurrying for signs in a confusing and dangerous environment. Power is raw, individual, and feudal; it is marked by loyalties of blood and iron and ready to be smeared by betrayal and ambition at any turn.

One of my first clues to this chasm in values that illuminates the Fall of Politics came shortly after I moved to the Pacific Northwest in 1990. I learned then that things we wore as badges of honor in Washington—the mocking of the public; the underlying belief that the right thing is whatever you can get away with; tolerance and acceptance of practices abhorred elsewhere (such as how to swindle a lobbyist out of a campaign contribution)—were considered grounds for being hanged from the nearest lamppost in the rest of America.

I was explaining "Budget Day" to a group of people at Portland State University. "Imagine," I recalled with fond memory. "Every policy wonk is reeling from overload caused by toxic exposure to budget numbers. Legislative alchemists all over town are scrounging through the massive budget document, plugging numbers into computers, running analyses and cross-analyses. And press secretaries like me? We're trying to decide whether to have the roast beef sub or Chinese carryout for lunch. Legislative directors and policy wonks are paid to understand things. Press secretaries are paid to understand complicated people. Give me three things from the budget I can use, and I'll gin up enough quotes to keep us in the news all week."

By the time I had finished the anecdote, I was laughing so hard I didn't look at the listeners' faces until I was done.

I was the only one laughing.

One woman stood up silently and walked away. Others stared coldly. Everyone else looked at me as if I were from another planet. I suddenly realized I was. A friend tactfully changed the subject to Wolf's Prolegomena on the Homeric Question.

I now look back on my experience in Washington for the answer to an urgent question: How do those in Washington politics solve the problem of the Fall of Politics, that separation of the political culture from the rest of society?

Here's a start: We cannot reinvent government without first reinventing the government and political culture itself. It's not a policy problem, it's not a process problem, and it's not a number-crunching problem. It's an inner issue—I would not venture to call

it a problem—on the individual human level. Reinventing government without reinventing the political culture is like giving breast
implants to a cardiac patient: all you do is pretty up the corpse. The
political world is made up of very human, deeply flawed people
who act out on the playing field of American democracy their fears,
desires, broken dreams, and dashed hopes. It is a wasted landscape
scraped clean of anything beyond self-interest and appetite. "You
need a metaphor," a former Capitol Hill staff director told me, "for
a guy who'll eat the other guy's leg off."

Our solution, then, lies not in "reinventing" the government
but in instigating change within *homo politicus*. It's a problem as old
as humanity. As Joni Mitchell wrote in the song "Woodstock,"
"We've got to get back to the garden." And she wasn't talking
about a Renaissance weekend, where elitist yuppies pat themselves
on the back over how bright they are before going back to the
upper reaches of the Clinton administration. They are convinced
they have no illusions about the world, but they have every illusion
about themselves.

We didn't want it that way. Bill Clinton was the one with the
promises, the one who made a devil's bargain with his rhetoric of
meaning and the politics of deliverance and who convinced
enough of us that he just might be different, that he was a spiritual
man who would use the dark arts of politics on our behalf instead
of against us.

He was the one, in the end, who lied.

And what does this have to do with my old buddy Jean-Jacques?

We are living in the twilight of the Enlightenment, in a time
when reason is on the run, when opinion instantly becomes faith
and faith becomes unshakable belief. The irrationalism has even
spread to science, which is under attack by multiculturalists, radical environmentalists, and feminist theorists. Written text, the
technological means of Enlightenment communication, is on the
run too. We are shifting rapidly to a visually based, multimedia-

dependent iconographic culture; nothing has accelerated the transition from the age of reason to a New Romanticism more than the computer. As Yale computer scientist David Gelerntner wrote in the *New Republic*, "While we bemoan the decline of literacy, computers discount words in favor of pictures and pictures in favor of video. While we worry about basic skills, we allow into the classroom software that will do a student's arithmetic or correct his spelling."

At the same time, the overload of the information highway has led us, ironically, back to the village path. There is simply too much information. In response, people no longer (if they ever) engage in rational, reasoned discourse. They have Conversations about Stories, which the media generate and lock into archetypal morality plays. In the environment of the Story, repetition builds roots that are difficult to dislodge even if the facts of the Story prove false—something every political consultant knows by now. Media stories today are often couched in terms of competing stark images—but why some work and some don't depends on the ability to connect with an underlying archetypal story of our culture and society.

The overload is not good, because there is a fundamental trouble in this land. Things are not getting better in the body politic or the family. "The crisis we face is now so deep and the transformation required so fundamental that real change can sometimes feel impossible," author Jim Wallis wrote. Too many of us are reaching the age where we begin to learn what everyone else before us grimly knew: that this body will betray and die, and always much too soon. A friend's brother dies of cancer at the age of thirty-eight. Tony, a longtime family friend, dead of leukemia at thirty-five. Your loved ones betray, too; there is no anguish more intolerable than the look on a little boy's face when his parents tell him they "are divorcing"; in the etiquette of these psychotherapeutic times, you cannot tell him that one parent sought the dissolution of the family in order to start "living by my feelings." You construct a wall, and the fate of children becomes its bricks. Families crumble, children's worlds break down by self-seeking New Agers, political abuses continue to run rampantly—all under the lash of the New Romanticism and the latter-day celebration of the self that began with the nineteenth-century Romantic movement and is continuing today under the guise of the psychotherapeutic culture and its language.

Thank you, Jean-Jacques Rousseau.

So as individuals and as a society, we find ourselves again on the great circle of Nietzsche's abyss. There is no transcendent secular salvational experience, politics or otherwise. Politics as salvation is nothing but fraud. The Enlightenment is over, and we have killed it by hand. We hope because we have no other choice, and the Clintons's greater fraud was to make the corpse dance.

Nowhere is this sense of the impending end of the *ancien régime* seen more vividly than in our nation's capital. Washington today is under Malcolm Lowry's volcano. It is the last days of the Raj, the spas of Pompeii, Berlin in the early '30s, drunk on itself and on a coast-to-coast bender.

According to press reports, the official portrait business is booming in Washington. Big oil paintings go for about twenty-eight grand a pop, and you don't even have to be famous. Andrew Card, who served eleven months as transportation secretary, had his Big One done (and didn't like it, either). Former Clinton agriculture secretary Mike Espy, forced out on ethics allegations, cut his price to a mere $12,500. Other Clinton cabinet secretaries, shedding the rhetoric of the new meritocracy, have also had no qualms about having their portraits done, too, along with most Democratic committee chairs, Speakers of the House, and other political handymen. The visage of power is so important in Washington that when John Deutch became Clinton's director of central intelligence, he had aides pester the manager of the Palm restaurant until Deutch's caricature was hung alongside the other thousand or so lobbyists, fixers, bagmen, and party hacks that adorn the restaurant's walls.

Legend has it that Roadtrip once offered to "drop trou" and provide a subsequent photocopy for the wall of his favorite restaurant, but he would neither confirm nor deny the rumor.

Benders? Did we say benders?

The president's wife goes from one guru to another, first with Michael "Politics of Meaning" Lerner and then with Hollywood spiritmeister Marianne Williamson. The First Lady vociferously denied the "guru" charge in an April 1995 letter to *Esquire* magazine, one of the first to publish a report about Williamson's visits. In the letter, Hillary blamed the report on a "religious right" with a hidden political agenda. She once again offered herself up as a national martyr for having reached out to so many people from so many walks of life, and then described herself as a "Christian witness" who would continue to "try to do the best I can to help the president and make my own contribution to the nation."

As for that contribution, Roadtrip quipped that Hillary could best make it "by staying on tour in the Third World until after the 1996 election and by shutting the hell up."

CHAPTER SEVEN

MONEY

Huge numbers of people are alienated, maybe as much as two-thirds of the public. They're angry that government spending is out of control, that public policy is bought and sold by insiders, and nothing they can do will change it.
—Republican strategist Gordon Black
in *Newsweek*, 15 September 1995

"Bet your ass they can't."
—Roadtrip, 21 November 1995

WASHINGTON IS A DRUG because power is the most virulent toxin of them all. People with a full head of the stuff express themselves in three major venues: money, sex, and clout. Along the way, normal and ordinary character flaws become magnified by the pressure and limelight. The flaws grow in proportion to the degree of success enjoyed by the given *homo politicus*. In the legislative area in particular, the flaws can grow to the point where they become the dominant character elements. All too often, staff can come to be seen as servants—which, for the purpose of political and legislative activities, they are.

This is Roadtrip's own version of a unified field theory of Washington politics. It's been through a number of versions over the years, notably what the rest of us called the "weekend version" and the "weekday version."

On the surface, this may not seem any different from IBM, or the behind-the-poolhouse couplings at your local suburban neighborhood association. But IBM, at least, produces a product. In Washington, there is no product—except the power itself. Money, sex, and clout are different faces of power. "Mirrors onto the godhead," Roadtrip would pontificate.

"Which one is most important?" I asked.

"That's a question no one in this town would ask on his own," he replied. "It's like saying what's more important, your left ventricle or your right auricle? It's all your heart, and none of them works without the other. Those things are in Washington's heart, too. We need them all."

I'd put my money on money. Clout is too vague. Sex? I know too many women who are supremely frustrated with a male population so concerned with access, prestige, and job-climbing they can't spare time for a relationship. Besides, nowhere is the Fall of Politics more evident than when you lift up the rocks of money and see what scurries from the shadows underneath.

Let's take a look at how Roadtrip's theory works in real life.

State of the Union speech, 24 January 1995. Bill Clinton's political back was to the wall. He and his brilliantly credentialed yuppie pros had just presided over the greatest Democratic electoral debacle of the twentieth century. He had responded by calling the public "political couch potatoes" at a speech to the Democratic National Committee a few days before. That approach went over well at the DNC, which was in a state of stunned denial anyway. The voters had just flushed forty years of big-government Democratic liberalism down the toilet, and the hacks had no answers. The average loss in an incumbent president's first term has been thirteen in the House and none in the Senate. Clinton, by comparison, presided over a loss of eight seats in the Senate and fifty-two in the House, including incumbent House Speaker Thomas Foley (D-Wash.) and three Democratic committee chairmen. No incumbent Republican senator or House member had lost; two incumbent Democratic senators and thirty-five House incumbents had been defeated. (The landing for Foley and the others will be soft; it's not like they just got laid off from a real job at AT&T. Foley's congressional pension will be an estimated $124,000 per year. The committee chairs will receive about $96,000 a year.)

The rout had been decisive.

As Washington analyst Michael Barone wrote in the *Almanac of American Politics*, "A clearer repudiation of the party in power cannot be imagined. Wherever history is headed, it is no longer headed left." Roadtrip offered that "voters were running away from the Democrats faster than that crowd in Thailand was chasing that Texas faith healer out of the country."

It was open season on Clinton. Former Republican White House aide Lyn Nofziger observed that "the 1994 elections were basically a civilian revolt not so much against big government but against Bill Clinton personally. The average American thinks Bill Clinton is a scumbag—he's dishonest, unethical, talks a great game, and doesn't live up to it, that he's a lying, draft-dodging son of a bitch."

His sentiments were echoed by defeated Senate candidate Dave McCurdy (D-Okla.), who had been highly critical of Clinton in his Senate bid. At a post-election address to the moderate Democratic Leadership Council (DLC), McCurdy said that "Bill Clinton won as a moderate, a new Democrat... but he has governed as something else.... While Bill Clinton has the mind of a new Democrat, he retains the heart of an old Democrat. The result is an administration that has pursued elements of a moderate and liberal agenda at the same time, to the great confusion of the American people." McCurdy urged the council to find someone other than Clinton, someone who was more loyal to moderate views. "It was a national referendum on Bill Clinton," McCurdy said. "The last three weeks, the dam broke and there was nothing we could do."

Joel Kotkin, editor of the Democratic Leadership Council's *New Democrat* magazine, went further. Citing a "betrayal" of moderate Democrats by Clinton, Kotkin argued that "new Democrats" needed to flat-out cut their ties to the president and break with liberal ideologues in the White House staff such as George Stephanopoulos, Harold Ickes, and Hillary Rodham Clinton. He even suggested it was time to consider leaving the Democratic party altogether.

At the State of the Union address, Clinton seemed unfazed. He delivered an extended lecture to Congress on ethics, gift-taking, and propriety in general. He seemed to chide congressional Democrats for giving him the tax increase he had sought. Bill Clinton was resorting to a tried and true tactic: running against himself. In Arkansas, he had run against his own record to regain the governor's mansion; he would do it again in the fall of 1995, outraging voters (because it wasn't true), Republicans (because it seemed to work), and the congressional Democrats (because they were left holding the bag).

In late January 1995, however, Clinton's belief that he should be given the remarkable ability to shed his skin on any convenient log was astonishing. He had presided over the most voracious fundraising machine in the history of the Democratic National Committee. His reliance on "soft" money, ostensibly given to national parties for voter registration and party-building, but actually targeted internally to specific races, was notorious. "Just like campaign contributions," laughed Roadtrip, who had bundled his share of bucks along the way. "Imagine that!"

"We have a lot more to do before people really trust the way things work around here," Clinton lectured. "Three times as many lobbyists are in the streets and corridors of Washington as were here twenty years ago. The American people look at their capital, and they see a city where the well connected and the well protected can work the system, but the interests of ordinary citizens are left out." Clinton had neglected to mention a certain lobbyist in the corridors of the White House, Harold Ickes, on whom Clinton had bestowed a coveted White House pass while Ickes was still a lobbyist for Puerto Rico. (Ickes is now deputy White House chief of staff.)

"As the new Congress opened its doors, lobbyists were still doing business as usual—the gifts, the trips—all the things that people are concerned about haven't stopped," Clinton continued. "Twice this month you missed opportunities to stop these practices. I know there were other considerations in those votes, but I want to use something that I've heard my Republican friends say from time to time: There doesn't have to be a law for everything."

Wild applause rang out from the Democratic corner, led by the late Commerce Secretary Ron Brown. (As Reagan aide Lyn Nofziger once said, Brown was "a very delightful sleazeball... there's nothing self-righteous about him at all.") Brown's death in Croatia naturally evoked mourning, but Brown was Washington to his fingertips. His integrity had been a subject for debate when fourteen Republican senators had written a letter to U.S. Attorney General Janet Reno urging her to investigate the charges made by Rep. William F. Clinger (R-Pa.), chairman of the House Government Reform and Oversight Committee, that Brown had fudged congressional testimony about his ties to a communications company that had, in turn, stiffed the Federal Deposit Insurance Corporation (FDIC) on a loan. The senators also accused Brown of having his business partner pay his personal bank debts of $190,000 in the summer of 1994. (This would help the secretary to avoid the tax liability of paying in cash.)

"We don't have to wait for legislation to pass to send a strong signal to the American people that things are really changing," Clinton continued. "But I also hope you will send me the strongest possible lobby reform bill, and I'll sign that, too. We should require lobbyists to tell the people for whom they work, what they're spending, what they want. We should also curb the role of big money in elections by capping the cost of campaigns and limiting the influence of PACs."

After a couple of swipes at conservative-dominated talk radio, he wrapped up that part of the speech with a tone of wounded outrage: "When the last Congress killed political reform last year, it was reported that the lobbyists actually stood in the halls of this sacred building and cheered. This year, let's give the folks back home something to cheer about."

My telephone rang the minute the president stopped talking. "The state of the Union might be sound, but the state of Clinton is in sorry damn shape," Roadtrip chortled. "Unless, of course, you're talking about raising special interest campaign money from all those lobbyists he just denounced. He's way ahead of everyone else." He'd have to do well to beat his own record on "soft" money. In 1992, Clinton had cruised into the presidency on the back of over $29 million in special-interest "soft" money contributions to the Democratic National Committee. They were gearing up for a repeat performance even as Bubba blubbered on about reform.

"Are you calling from the halls of that sacred building?" I asked him.

"Damn right I am," he replied. "And before I came over I had to drop off a couple of sacred political action committee checks to a couple of sacred members, including those holier-than-thou sacred Republican freshmen. I love sacred freshmen, especially reformers. They understand the state and local game, and it's great to watch them take their first elbow to the cheekbone. Welcome to the NBA, baby! Now I'm going to have a couple of sacred stiff ones and figure out ways to make even more tainted lucre if I'm lucky."

Roadtrip had a point here. During the November 1995 budget deliberations, freshman Rep. Mark Souder (R-Ind.) told the *New York Times*, "We didn't come here to raise debt limits." Raising political action committee money, however, was another question entirely. The freshmen might have vowed to change Washington, but money was not part of the deal. Nine freshmen received over $100,000 in PAC money in the first six months of 1995: Reps. John Ensign (R-Nev.), Daniel Frisa (R-N.Y.), Jon Christensen (R-Nebr.), Charles Norwood (R-Ga.), Greg Ganske (R-Iowa), Randy Tate (R-Wash.), Frank Cremeans (R-Ohio), Thomas Davis (R-Va.), and Brian Bilbray (R-Calif.).

As veteran Washington lobbyist Howard Marlowe posted on his Internet site, "Look for PACs to be around Washington for a long time, getting more and more entrenched with each new Congress." House GOP Chairman Bill Paxon bragged in November 1995 that the *average* freshman received over $60,000 from PACs, proving once again that greed is bipartisan.

The same thing goes for politics. Budget-cutting freshman Mark Neumann (R-Wis.) put federal spending through a fine-tooth comb—except when he added a provision to the defense spending bill that would have forced the Navy to buy generators from Coltec Industries. Coltec is in Neumann's district, and its prices are higher than other bidders. The Navy had complained that the measure would increase costs and lower efficiency, but to no avail.

"Call them what you want," Roadtrip enthused, admiringly, "but those folks know how to play the game." Rep. Linda Smith (R-Wash.) echoed his view in a 20 August 1995 speech to United We Stand America: "I watched my freshmen colleagues have to come up against a system that just will eat you up." She said, "I want to tell you what was scary to me as I watched these idealists one by one face something that they could not get around. Their opponents had been raising PAC money, and many of these challengers had to go with a big debt to Washington. And guess who was at the door to pay the debt? The special interests."

Thirty-six House incumbents in 1992 had spent more than $1 million apiece in pursuit of reelection. The bulk of the money came from PACs. Ironically, the most egregious were the supposed leaders of campaign finance reform, including Democratic Caucus Chairman Steny Hoyer (D-Md.); Rep. Martin Frost (D-Tex.), the House "leader" of campaign finance reform; and Chief Deputy Whip David Bonior (D-Mich.). All of them had advocated a $600,000 spending cap. Overall, only forty-five challengers raised even half of what their incumbent opponents did. The response of then-House Speaker Thomas Foley in February 1993 was to back-slide on his 1992 pledge of fast action to clean up campaign financing (which contributed in no small part to his thrashing at the polls in 1994). Foley insisted during post-election discussions with President Clinton that not only would he not commit to a specific timetable, but that no reform of any kind would go into effect until 1996. (OOPS—he missed it by two years. Oh well.)

Greed—it's not just a Republican trait, as Robert Rubin, President Clinton's top economic adviser and former chairman of Goldman, Sachs, and Company, demonstrated further when he wrote and sent a letter in December 1992 to ask his clients to continue their relationship with his firm, encouraging them to communicate with him at the White House. "I also look forward to continuing to work with you in my new capacity," concluded a letter to a Japanese client that was printed in the *New York Times*.

To put it bluntly, many of the Clintonistas, on close inspection, could have been mascots for the Era of Greed—i.e., the Republican eighties. Zoe Baird lost her shot at being the first female attorney general for not paying Social Security taxes for two illegal aliens she'd employed. None of Clinton's Washington insiders smelled a problem until public opinion weighed in against Baird. Federal Judge Kimba Wood (what's with it with these yuppie names—Zoe, Kimba—and can "Caitlin" be far behind?) lost out because she, too, had hired illegal immigrants. No surprise, Ron Brown admitted on 7 February 1993, that he, too, had evaded Social Security taxes on his maid's wages. Contributions to freshmen increased so much, in fact, that they helped push overall donations to House incumbents 34 percent to $45.5 million in the first six months of 1995.

"What's the crowd saying about all this criticism by Clinton?" I asked Roadtrip.

"Make a circle with your right thumb and forefinger. Join your other three fingers at that point, too. Aim it at a picture of the president and make it go up and down real fast."

Eschewing TV commentary, Roadtrip continued with his on-the-spot reporting.

"They were toasting him and Hillary at the bar at the Democratic Club a few minutes ago," he said. "I saw four of 'em knock down shots of Makers Mark to the cheering huzzahs of 'this sacred building!' The next one was to 'that sacred bitch!,' followed by the names of everyone in the Clinton administration who'd ever shaken them down for money, in or out of the administration. But when they started toasting Paula Jones and the Whitewater creepy crawlies, I figured the crowd would turn mean and ugly in a hurry. They might be smiling, but when their eyes turn into slits and they start muttering to no one in particular, the smart money hits the road."

He was headed for the Capitol Hill Club, the Republican redoubt.

"Republicans have good manners and even better liquor," he noted.

I checked in with another buddy in the trade. "Scoop" represents natural resources–based interests and has strong Democratic ties that have weathered the worst of the Clinton administration's assault. Clinton's State of the Union broadside against lobbyist and influence peddlers, however, was too much. Scoop was taking it personally.

"You know, I've really had it with that guy," Scoop pouted. "There doesn't have to be a law for everything! Where does he

think his goddamn money comes from? I'll tell you where—
FROM PEOPLE LIKE US, THAT'S WHO!"

Two weeks after the State of the Union Address, the *Wall Street Journal* would ask, "Did Ron Brown testify truthfully to Congress when he said there was no link between Corridor [his broadcasting company] and First International [a communications company]? Was Mr. Brown a participant in a scheme to defraud the FDIC and RTC? Did Mr. Brown falsify his financial disclosure forms (a felony) to conceal some of these transactions?"

The *Wall Street Journal* raised some good questions, and good answers were not forthcoming. We will probably never know now and Brown of course cannot defend himself. But at the time, it was a fair question. Had Brown pocketed $412,000 in 1993 from the sale of First International—in which he had neither invested any money nor spent any time running it? Were $277,000 of the $412,000 involved the forgiving of a Brown debt of $277,000?

"I'm in the wrong business," Scoop moaned when he heard the news. "Where did I go wrong?"

You could hear the echoes of Bill's plea: ...there doesn't have to be a law... just stop taking the lobbyists' perks, just stop... still doing business as usual.... This, of course, was only the tip of the iceberg.

"The Clinton administration and even Bill himself might be saying and doing a lot of things about ethics, congressional reform, lobbying, and influence-peddling, but stopping it is not one of them and had never been a Clinton priority in the first place," Roadtrip said, and then added, "Thank God."

CHAPTER EIGHT

SEX

IT'S DIFFICULT at best to consider the role of sex in Washington politics. Remember Robert Redford's remark during the filming of *All the President's Men*—that Washington makes Hollywood look like a convent?

Believe it or not, sex did not come to town with Bill Clinton, though our president who, according to Hunter S. Thompson, has "the midnight taste of a man who might go out on a double-date with the Rev. Jimmy Swaggart" has certainly contributed to the notion of our capital as a haven of horniness. But Washington's public sex stories are only the tip of the iceberg—Clinton and Gennifer Flowers, Clinton and Paula Jones Corbin, Clinton and half of Arkansas. There are countless other Washington sex stories that aren't as well known beyond the Beltway. One of my favorites has Senators Ted Kennedy and Christopher Dodd,

Kennedy's Sancho Panza, partying it up in Central America with a covey of young ladies, all walking down a secluded beach, naked as jaybirds. Some Washington sex stories have odd only-in-Washington endings: Donna Rice, for example. The Miami model, whose liaison with Gary Hart derailed Hart's 1988 presidential campaign, is back in town. She's working as a lobbyist. Her cause? Banning pornography on the Internet. Go figure.

As a public service, I did a quick poll of the old Capitol Hill gang for their best-remembered Washington sex stories. All the best ones (read: most embarrassing), however, seemed to stem from one particular extended circle of Democratic political operatives, members, staffers, and lobbyists. So we'll just take it from the top and follow the trail to wherever it leads us.

Once upon a time, there was a pretty young wife of a newly elected Democratic congressman from Texas. She had a strong sexual appetite, which by most accounts she had already begun to satisfy outside the bounds of holy matrimony and before her husband gained a seat in Congress. Several months after their arrival in Washington, a staffer was assigned to accompany her to a fundraising event back in the district. The staffer from Washington found himself waiting outside his hotel for her to pick him up.

"You ready to party?" she grinned as she swung to the curb in a sports car. The aide knew the sports car did not belong to her or her husband, who was back in Washington.

Uh-oh, he thought as he glanced at her skimpy outfit.

"Here," she announced a few minutes later over the blare of the radio and pulled into a convenience store parking lot. "You wait here." He did. She returned in a minute with a cold six-pack of malt liquor tall boys, cracked open two, handed him one, and drank half of hers before they left the parking lot. A dry Texas wind howled through the open windows as they drove at high speed to the local bar, where a political gathering was in progress.

Burping malt liquor, the staffer hastily excused himself and went to the restroom. He found a pay phone and frantically dialed the congressman's staff director, his boss, at home. "What in the hell is going on down here?!" he demanded. "This crazy blonde is downing malt liquor like it's going out of style. Now she's drinking tequila at the bar, and I think I saw a pack of condoms at the bottom of the paper bag that had the malt liquor. Just what the hell am I supposed to do?"

"Well, don't fuck her, for starters," the staff director chuckled. "Look, protect yourself," the voice of wisdom from Washington continued. "Stay at the bar as long as you can. Don't let her drink and drive, if you can help it. Get lots of people into that final good-bye conversation. Call yourself a taxi back to the hotel. And get her in a cab if you can."

"But what if I can't?!"

"You're paid to think on your feet."

The staffer returned to the raucous group at the bar, which by now was deeply engaged in recounting political war stories. The Congressman's wife had slowed her drinking, and the staffer breathed a sigh of relief.

"Come on," she shrieked suddenly, grabbing him by the arm, "we're goin' dan-cin!" His protests did little good. Within minutes they were roaring across town to a Texas-sized country music dance hall.

Jeezus, he muttered as they walked into a huge crowd. *I don't dance and I can't dance to country music. Worse, in a crowd this big someone is going to recognize us.*

"Let's git us a drink," she suggested, steering him toward one of the long bars at either end of the circular dance floor.

Oh no, he thought. *His career in politics flashed before his eyes.* They approached the bar and bought yet another round of drinks.

"Well, fancy meeting you here!" the wife exclaimed in a loud voice, as she gave a big hug to a tall stranger. The staffer saw the look that passed between them—it was like a Panhandle heat wave—and heaved a huge sigh of relief.

"I think I'm going to check out the action over there," he told her, pointing to a group of young women dressed like Dallas Cowboy cheerleaders.

"See ya!" she yelled. The last sight he had was of her backside sliding into the front seat of a Porsche.

Time to call Washington again. This time the staff director, awakened from a sound sleep, was less amused.

"Look," the Texas custodian wailed, "she's still drinking. We're at some goddamn cow palace. And she's just taken off with some cowboy in a Porsche!"

"Great!" replied the voice of wisdom from Washington.

"Great? Great! What do you mean, great?"

"She's not driving drunk, and you're not with her. Better yet, you're not fucking her."

"You're goddamn right I'm not fucking her! Will you give that a rest?! And how is that great?"

"Because," the staff director sagely replied, "it's gonna go bad. All these political affairs go bad. Believe me, I've been on both sides of that game before. And when it goes bad, someone goes down, and when you're talking a member or the member's wife, it's rarely one of them that goes down. You did good, boy. Now either get some of your own there or go back to your hotel. And don't call back."

He went back to his hotel, but that wasn't the end of *l'affaire blonde wife*. Within a year, the same staffer found himself back in the office annex. The annex held the sophisticated computer equipment that kept files on every voter in the district and had the ability to unleash a barrage of computer-generated mail to constituents.

The computer operator was shooting the breeze with his assistant, who had a small crowd transfixed with an extremely graphic description of his roommate's sex life—which on the evening before, had included an apartment-wide romp with the very same blonde wife from Texas.

A year or so later, the congressman and the blonde wife are divorced. The staff in the main office are gathering around the coffee machine, trading the usual lost weekend stories.

"Well, I certainly wouldn't do it," one woman snapped with disgust.

"Now that's an interesting observation, Clarice," replied the veteran of the earlier predicament in Texas. "Don't know that I ever contemplated the possibility that there was anything you wouldn't do."

"Like oral sex in 1789?" Clarice retorted, referring to a swanky restaurant with a date for a name.

"Did they do that back then?"

"Yes, you idiot, they probably did, and in fact I'm sure they did, people being what they are, but that doesn't mean His Lardness has to do it in the goddamn restaurant!" she said referring to her esteemed boss. (You may think His Lardness is Teddy Kennedy. He's not. There are tons of horny fat guys on the Hill.)

Now that in fact shut the staffer up. The member was known by many fond nicknames by his staff, His Lardness and His Immenseness being two of the more kindly appellations, and the thought of him engaging in flirtations, especially at a restaurant like 1789 was revolting.

The veteran shivered and said, "You've got to be kidding."

"Would I kid about something like that? That's disgusting!"

"With who? And how?"

"Well, let's take a guess. First they had a bunch of drinks—"

"Who had a bunch of drinks?"

"The congressman and that lobbyist I can't stand."

"Ah-ha."

"Ah-ha, my ass. Then they went to the restaurant and had

more drinks, of course. Then they tell the waiter to take his time bringing the food. *Then* they draw the privacy curtain across the booth—"

"Why do you think they had the curtain in the first place?"

"Not for that!" Clarice spat. She added, "Then they went at it."

"And how are you so sure?"

"Because," the woman staffer sitting next to her interrupted with laughter, "I was having dinner with a date right across the aisle from them!"

"What can she see in him?" the disgusted Clarice demanded.

"What can she not see in him?" the witness laughed. "The son of a bitch is 300 pounds!"

Another vignette of sex in Washington involves the staff director for a member of Congress from the mid-Atlantic region. Let's call him Harry. Harry never let his marriage get in the way of a good time and that included an occasional but substantial drug habit. So one night he leaves work after calling his wife to say that he'll be late because he has to pick up a friend at the bus station. He goes to the downtown bus station and meets his source to pick up his drugs. A thousand dollars later or so, he decides to have a couple of drinks. He goes to a bar. There he runs into, completely by accident, an intern from his office and her twin sister. Both are young, blonde, and very attractive. A few more drinks later, and Harry suggests that the three of them and his jacket full of partying material go find a nearby motel. The women readily agree, and they spend the rest of the night together in a state of what Harry would later term "pure debauchery." Harry finally passes out.

Hours later, Harry awakens in a panic. He looks at the clock. It's a quarter till seven. "Shit!!" he yells, throwing on his clothes. His alarm clock back home always goes off at 7 A.M. sharp, and he knows he has to beat it and get in before his wife wakes up.

Driving like a maniac and weaving through traffic, Harry finally arrives home. He shuts off the engine and unlocks the front door with what he hopes is nothing less than stealth technology.

His wife is walking down the hallway toward the door, furious, to say the least. Harry makes an attempt to pull himself together (and he looks bad, really bad), and then he says nonchalantly, "So the bus was late?"

Maybe the sex itself isn't any different, after all, from say IBM. But people in politics have a strange sense of history. They not only have sex, they keep diaries about it. Unfortunately for them (and fortunately for us), these enjoyable scribblings are always landing in the hands of troublesome people such as reporters or special prosecutors. For senators there's always Senator Bob Packwood's infamous diary. According to Bob, at precisely 6:30 P.M. on Sunday, 2 February 1992, Packwood had a telephone conversation with Elaine Franklin, his chief of staff. The senator's "dear diary" noted:

I said, are you seeing [deleted] this week? She says, well, I'm not sure. I said, well, you've seen him the last two Thursdays. Is he coming to town this week? She says, well, I'm not sure of that. I says, well, if he comes to town, are you going to see him? She says, probably.

Now what are you and I going to do now that we have this professional relationship? I said, what are we going to do at night when we're in Portland?

She said, well, we'll have to see. And I said, in this professional relationship, I haven't seen anybody so far. You've made love to [deleted] twice. I said, by the way, did you use a condom? You told me I had to use a condom if I made love to other women, and you said you'd use a condom if you made love to [deleted], or he would.

She said, that was before that Wednesday evening. I said, [deleted], I apologized about that several times. She said, I've got to do something about your drinking.

And I'll wager I'm not going to spend any time at her house on the next trip, and she's not going to spend any time at the Red Lion, and we probably won't make love. But it's just as well. I haven't got a lot of time to worry about all the other women in terms of making love. If it comes along, fine. I haven't got time to worry about it. I've got time to worry about this primary.

Now, you might think that all of these sexual shenanigans were brought to an abrupt halt by the 1994 election by those hard-charging, reform-minded, sleep-in-their-office Republican freshmen. But you would be wrong.

Consider the case of freshman Republican John Shadegg, who *should* have slept in his office.

Shadegg (R-Ariz.) was elected to Congress from Arizona's most conservative congressional district. He was a family values kind of guy who told the *New York Times* right after the election, "I don't want to become a Washingtonian. I have a twelve-year-old and a nine-year-old to get home to.... I'm going to do everything I can to resist those trappings of power because I think they do corrupt you."

Once in Washington, Mr. Shadegg saw things differently. He was quickly elected an assistant whip in the Republican leadership. He was appointed to the powerful House Budget Committee and the Government Reform and Oversight Committee. He became a member of the Sportsmen's Caucus, where he went on to specialize in the world's oldest indoor sport. Shadegg soon was caught "in mid-yelp," as one witty lobbyist put it, with Meredith Stewart Maxfield, the wife of fellow Republican freshman Jon Christensen of Nebraska. Mr. Christensen himself was the artful trapper. According to one account, Christensen punched Shadegg and a fistfight ensued in front of the wife, who was naked throughout the fisticuffs. The episode is said to have reflected negatively on Shadegg's "family values" image back in Arizona. But never mind. Shadegg could always follow a time-honored Washington tradition and become... a lobbyist.

CHAPTER NINE

INFLUENCE

BACK TO MONEY NOW.

Politicians have to raise it from somewhere. In Washington that means lobbyists. Unfortunately, that's the good news about lobbyists.

The bad news is that politicians are now breeding lobbyists. Literally. It's so bad that the Associated Press reported on this phenomenon in 1994. Some of the more egregious examples of this new species:

Robin Dole, daughter of Senate Majority Leader and presidential contender Robert Dole, hustles the Hill for Century 21 Real Estate.

Jamie L. Whitten, son of the former House Appropriations Committee chairman, owns a lobbying firm that specializes in obtaining federal money for clients from that same committee.

Michelle Clay, daughter of former civil rights movement fire-brand William Clay, who was chairman of the House Post Office and Civil Service Committee before the Republican takeover, is also a lobbyist. Guess her favorite committees.

Clifford Gibbons, son of House Ways· and Means Committee Chairman Sam Gibbons, routinely brings his lobbying clients before his father's committee. This even bothered fellow lobbyist Wright Andrew, who told the Associated Press, "I've seen situations where there were clear conflicts.... I've seen people get information nobody else could get—drafts, confidential stuff—and where people would use them merely because of the connection." In one celebrated instance of lobbying skill, young Cliff introduced the chairman of Mutual Life Insurance Company to his father at lunch in the private members' dining room in the Capitol building.

Roadtrip was unimpressed. "Sam Gibbon's been for sale for so long that the only thing Cliff can do for you is get a family discount," he scoffed.

Such inside relationships, however, are important to the rest of us because lobbyists have enormous influence over how we live. According to the journalists Bartlett and Steele, "...the triumph of special interests... determines whether you have a job that pays $15 an hour or one that pays $6; whether you have a pension and health care insurance; whether you can afford to own a home. It governs everything from the tax system to imports of foreign goods, from the bankruptcy system to regulatory oversight."

PAC worship is completely bipartisan. In 1995, Republicans were, according to the Center for Responsive Politics, the ones raking in the PAC dollars. An analysis done by the Center's Larry Makinson showed that two-thirds of the PAC contributions in the first half of 1995 went to the new Republican majority in Congress, a complete reversal from the 1993–94 election cycle. The bell-wether was unions, where twenty labor PACs actually gave more money to the new Republicans than to the Democrats.

Incumbency is the key to the PACs' generosity. But, as Roadtrip pointed out, it's a two-way street. "It's one thing to offer a PAC check," Roadtrip noted, "and another to accept it. Isn't it odd? Republicans don't seem to care where their PAC dollars come from. Republicans—gasp—were accepting money from the unions!"

Anything goes in Washington's crazy world. The Center study further showed that PACs contributed $35.2 million during the first six months of 1995 and $23.2 million went to Republicans. All told, almost 79 percent of all PAC contributions came from business, 14 percent came from labor, and only $1.7 million from ideological groups.

So who do you believe? Everybody's talking a different talk, and there's more spin than at a Frisbee convention. But look at the players:

House Speaker Newt Gingrich fronted for a $50,000 a plate fundraising dinner on 7 February 1995. The purpose was to raise money for a conservative television broadcasting company. Gingrich defended press criticism, naturally by claiming that Clinton had done the same thing for the Democratic National Committee; that made it all right for Newt.

Former Congressman Vin Weber, Gingrich confidante, a lobbyist as well as a Democrat, receiving $10,000 a month from the same Israeli free trade zone that hired Gingrich's wife Marianne at $2,500 a month, plus commissions.

Senate Majority Leader Bob Dole took to the airwaves the morning after Clinton's speech, terming Clinton's call for Congress to quit taking perks from lobbyists a "cheap shot." Dole pointed out correctly that Clinton had had no problem accepting money from those same special interests for his own legal defense fund in the Paula Jones matter and called Clinton's comments on lobbyists "probably the low point in his speech." "Let's face it, Mr. President," Dole asked on *Fox Morning News,* "have you seen a lobbyist lately? Probably have."

Dole himself is no stranger to lobbyists—in the family or otherwise. In his 1992 election, for example, he accepted $1,597,189 from PACs, which was more than one-half of all the money he raised that year.

Washington's political culture not only moved deftly to protect its sources of money, but it also worked to insulate itself from strong public demands for reform. Despite the success of the Contract with America in 1994, Gingrich rapidly backed off on the term limit issue. Republicans in both the House and Senate applied the pressure. It's tough to become rich and powerful when your days are numbered. Republicans, as well as Democrats, know this. According to an analysis by U.S. Term Limits, votes within the Republican conference on including term limits in the contract were "close and contentious." Rep. Dick Armey was able to prevail over Reps. Henry Hyde and Tom DeLay. The analysis, moreover, came only after data from pollster Frank Luntz showed support for the issue "was not only the highest among all issues asked, but could provide the difference in as many as 15 House races that November—possibly enough to make a difference between a solid Republican minority and the first Republican majority in 40 years." Gingrich was always lukewarm to term limits; in 1989, he told reporters that he wanted thirty-two more years in the House.

Wall Street Journal editorial writer John Fund, one of the founding fathers of the term limits movement, issued a warning on 10 February 1995. Fund first reported that incumbents of both parties were scheming to undermine term limits. He sternly opined, "We haven't seen an issue in a long time with deeper support than term limits. It's time for the GOP establishment to recognize that."

It may take a while. The 30 March 1995 Supreme Court defeat of the tough six-year term limits shows that it may take quite a while to recognize that term limits are essential to changing Washington. "Look, you gotta understand: term limits were a political tool with which to batter the House Democratic leadership when they were in the majority," a jaundiced House Republican leadership staffer explained. "It did its job in the late '80s and early '90s. Now we're in the driver's seat, and nobody wants to take his or her hand off the wheel. We haven't held power in forty years. Also, because of the attack strategy against Foley and the Democratic leadership, it was always a House thing. Dole and the Senate never bought it—and never will. They were perfectly willing to let us use it. But there's no way they're going to let us do it. Term limits never were and never will be about actually limiting the terms of members."

Not surprisingly, a number of observers are onto the Republicans. Scott Rasmussen of the Term Limits Leadership Council told *USA Today*, "Expecting members of Congress to put reasonable limits on themselves is like expecting a preschooler to give himself a reasonable bedtime—it's never going to happen."

"Hard to blame them, though," a Democratic staffer countered. "When Tip O'Neill sold American Express cards, Ronald Reagan made a million bucks for a speech to the Japanese, and Mario Cuomo is doing Dorito ads."

Defeated House Speaker Thomas Foley is currently treating the country to the spectacle of the fallen hero groveling for dollars as a—what else?—paid lobbyist for the law firm of Akin, Gump, Strauss, Hauer, and Feld. He also collects a congressional pension of about $124,000 a year.

Do you feel sorry for Foley? If so, put a dollar in an envelope and send it to him. Affix to it this coupon:

Poor Tom can't live on his congressional pension of $124,000 a year. So the man who was once second in the line of presidential succession now works on his knees, begging for money and favors as a lobbyist for a top Washington, D.C., influence-peddling law firm.

So let's help Tom and restore dignity to the Speakership at the same time by joining the 'Buck for Tom' program. Just tape a dollar bill (more if you're feeling flush), fold, and mail to Tom so he won't have to tarnish his former high office any more for money! It's easy! It's fun! And it's almost as cheap as Tom's reputation!

"We did a study at the start of the Clinton administration," said Charles Lewis of the Center for Public Integrity. "We found that two-thirds of the unpaid campaign advisers who carried so much weight with Clinton were from inside the Beltway. Clinton himself never promoted campaign finance reform until July 1992, when Perot, Buchanan, and Brown were gaining ground. Then on his first night in D.C. as president-elect, he was with Vernon Jordan, Ron Brown, and Bob Strauss, followed by his appearance at the $10,000 per table fundraiser at Union Station for lobbyists. From July 1992 to the transition, the message sent to lobbyists was, 'Hey, I'm one of you, don't worry.'"

This view is held by Susan Estrich, the *USA Today* columnist who was prominent in the Dukakis campaign. She wrote, "As a candidate for president, Bill Clinton promised to clean up the 'brain-dead' politics of Washington. But Democrats were unable to mobilize their own members to replace a system that favors incumbents."

Lewis continued: "When two of his top aides left to become lobbyists in the first six months of his administration, instead of declaring he was aghast, Clinton gave them a big hug in the Rose Garden. When campaign finance reform finally showed up, Clinton allowed Tom Foley to dictate the timing, which to me was the height of hypocrisy because Foley was an avowed opponent of anything that would upset the status quo."

I called Steve Stockmeyer, who heads the Ad Hoc PAC Coalition. He is a very engaging fellow and eager to help.

"You've got about 4,000 PACs today but almost none before 1974," he explained. "The landmark 1974 campaign finance reform legislation created an explosion of PACs that peaked in the mid-'80s. Today, about twelve million people nationwide participate in PACs. For as many as half or more, it's the only participation they do in the political system beyond voting. It's something that brings people into the system and promotes good citizenship."

"Like a political mutual fund?"

"Exactly," he replied approvingly. "I use the same term myself. It makes voices heard that are not heard. Besides, it's a healthy sign of American pluralism and the only part of the 1974 reforms that worked."

"How so?" I had never heard of any reform that actually worked.

"The parts that are in trouble are in the 'soft' money category. Party soft money is disclosed but limited. Nonparty soft money is not disclosed, and a lot of the liberal nonprofit groups go this route. The Sierra Club has an extensive grassroots political operation that identifies voters and then turns them out.

"Yeah, the Keating scandal gave us a glimpse of how that kind of thing could work," Stockmeyer continued. "Cranston set up voter registration drives with nonprofit organizations, and Keating put in $1.3 million. It became part of Cranston's political empire. See, you can go into a district and run a voter registration drive by neighborhood and get the voters you want."

"Slick."

"Yeah, not even the reform groups have recommended getting rid of that one because a lot of them engage in it. If Ralph Nader goes to a congressional district in election season, he'll denounce an incumbent for having a terrible consumer record. Who pays for this trip? His expenses? The public is told none of that. He just sort of shows up at key races around the country, and nobody's the wiser."

As an unnamed Washington lobbyist told the *National Journal* in July 1994, "You maintain and cultivate your relationships. You give money and help people and do favors whether you need them or not. It's just the way this city works.... [A $25,000 soft money donation] is nothing. I piss that away in a week."

"What about the reform legislation Clinton and Foley killed?" I asked.

"The current debate got started in 1986 with Senator David Boren's [D-Okla.] anti-PAC bill, then the Democratic leadership made it the standard Common Cause position," Stockmeyer explained. "Republicans didn't like it but their bills looked weak by comparison. Both parties painted themselves into corners. It was a PR game, not a legislative one. Both the Democrats and Republicans purposefully designed legislation not to pass but to get a PR advantage.

"Along comes Clinton with a strong commitment, on paper at least, to do campaign finance reform. Then he gets clobbered by the House Democrats, who tell him they were in a win-win situation. We get all the credit for reform with our bill, they said, but we still get the money. The White House caved and went with the traditional Democratic approach."

"Why'd they cave?"

"Clinton needed Congress. And it was a personal issue for each member. The House guys more than anyone else convinced the White House not to do anything. There was a meeting in March 1993. Foley's campaign finance reform lieutenant was Rep. Sam Gejdenson and his staff guy was Perry Pokios. They drew the line, and the White House put its tail between its legs. Clinton made an announcement about an outline of a bill, and I've never seen the tracks of the administration since."

"It's not all Clinton's fault," Stockmeyer continued. "He doesn't have a corner on hypocrisy. Look at all those members these days. They're bashing PACs on the floor by day and collecting the money at night. And the ones who swore off PACs are taking individual contributions from the same sources."

"To me," he sighed, "PACs are a victim of their own success. They're the most easily identifiable interest dollars. It's still difficult with individual contributions. So they're the most exposed politically. And they get hit up all the time for tribute payments from leadership members and committee chairs who don't need the money but raise it because they can. And a lot of campaign war chests are used to cover personal living expenses as well."

Stockmeyer had some good points, but I checked in with Road-trip—just in case.

"Now that's all well and good," Roadtrip told me when I recounted what I had heard. "In fact, I'll help. I'll just pick up the goddamn telephone and work my way through the Lobbyist Yellow Pages. Hello? Hello? What's the going rate for a meeting with [Deputy White House Chief of Staff] Harold Ickes? Do I hear five thou? Ten thou, you say? Cool. Check's in the mail. Have yours call mine. Ciao, baby."

In November 1994, somebody slipped *Roll Call* reporter Tim Burger a copy of an internal memo from the firm of Gold and Liebengood about how to peddle fancy dinners, gifts, and campaign contributions in return for access and influence. The memo was standard modus operandi for a Washington lobbying outfit. The story was picked up by news outlets across the country. Much wailing and gnashing of teeth followed.

Lobbyists aren't the end-all; they're middlemen, the fixers, the arrangers, the greasers of the skids. Washington is a town where money and power talk, and the lobbyists make the market. They cannot guarantee what you're going to find at the end of the skids, but on occasion they can bend the odds. They have been decidedly influential in maintaining Washington's pro-lobbyist PAC environment. A recent brochure by the National Association of Business Political Action Committees (NABPAC) states that it "backs and leads coalitions of corporate, association, labor and philosophical groups dedicated to preserving the role of PACs in the election process.... NABPAC sponsors studies by leading academics and national polls which provide objective analyses of election reform proposals and refute the negative image surrounding PACs." Special plaudits went to former Congressman Beryl Anthony, "who opened new doors for us on Capitol Hill and at the White House."

Ralph Nader was moved to ask on the Internet: "Will these

politicians actually give up the epicurean meals, luxurious vacations, golf, ski and tennis trips they enjoy?"

On 9 December 1995, Congress voted to change the way lobbying in Washington is regulated. The ranks of the 6,000 registered lobbyists would swell considerably under the new legislation to anywhere from 20,000 to 60,000 because the definition of what activities legally constitute lobbying was expanded. And a week before, the House voted on what appeared to be a tough curb on free meals, vacations, and other freebies from lobbyists.

A friend told me there might be a loophole in the new "reform" bill. I called Roadtrip. I told him there was talk of a loophole.

"Wrong."

"There's no loophole?"

"Of course there is, idiot. But we didn't find it. We put it there. It got there on purpose.

"Look at the bill. Read the goddamn language. It says that anything involving PAC activities are specifically exempt. That means not only can we take the members out for dinner, but we also have to give them a PAC check to make it all legal!"

Some folks around town were crowing in public. Wright Andrews, president of the American League of Lobbyists, was ecstatic. "The House ban, in particular, is going to have a big impact on the practice of taking members out to lunch," he told a reporter. "It will force a closer link between lobbying and campaigning. You'll be able to go out to lunch with a member, but instead of paying for his meal you'll be able to give him a campaign contribution."

"Look at the rest of the fine print," Roadtrip ordered merrily. "Members can still give speeches to conventions. Gosh, that means I get to fly an influential committee chairman to Hawaii instead of renting a room at the D.C. Hilton. That's my kind of reform, baby, my kind of reform. The members are no dummies, either. Did you see they exempted 'fact-finding' trips, too? That means every lob-

byist worth his PAC check is going to go into the fact-finding business. I'm already there. I'm working on it right now. And tell Ralph
Nader thanks again for me, okay?"

"Are you guys going to do the same thing to campaign finance
reform?" I asked.

"Look, let me clue you in on something: no one wants campaign
finance reform. OK, the goo-goos do [Roadtrip's term for good-
government types]. But no one else does. Not Clinton, not Gingrich, not Dole, not Gramm, not the RNC, not the DNC, not
business, not labor, not nobody. Remember the deal Gingrich just
cut on campaign reform?" Gingrich had announced in November
1995 that he would go along with President Clinton to set up a
commission to study campaign reform. The commission, however,
would not finish its work until after the 1996 election.

"You wouldn't believe what went into that behind the scenes,"
Roadtrip bragged. "Sure, it looked like Gingrich walked into the
committee room and on C-SPAN and said let's do the commission.
But it was coordinated with the White House all the way. And the
phone calls! Panetta to Gingrich. Gingrich to the RNC's [and Gingrich aide] Joe Gaylord. Back to Panetta. Panetta to his boys at the
DNC and the White House political shop. Harold Ickes going
psycho at the thought that something would get between him and
the federal limit [on raising campaign money] before the first of the
year. I'm telling you, they didn't need this many phone calls to start
the Persian Gulf War. The big boys on all sides were nerved.
When Gingrich agreed to the study, which essentially meant don't
do it until after the election, the smiles broke out everywhere—the
West Wing, the Speakers' Rooms, the campaigns. It meant lock
and load, we're going to get to go at each other with everything we
can get our hands on, and nobody can stop us."

The Democratic reaction was telling. For once, Gephardt and
Steny Hoyer, chair of the House Democratic Steering Committee,
lauded Gingrich. White House press secretary Mike McCurry,

usually a sharp-tongued critic of Gingrich, called the proposal "thoughtful." However, "The old boys and the establishment came together to stall for time," said Linda Smith of Washington, one of those raucous Republican freshmen.

"Let me give you the perfect metaphor for campaign finance reform," Roadtrip said. "*Newsweek* magazine just reported that a group of French artists in Paris decorate dog crap. I'm not making this up. They spot a pile of droppings and draw chalk outlines of plates, and put glasses, forks, knives, spoons, and so on next to the plate. Then they add real food like spaghetti. Now transfer that up to politics and campaign finance reform. It all looks good and pretty and laid out according to protocol. But it's shit at the core and will always be shit at the core."

"So how would you get rid of the money?"

"The money's not the fundamental problem," he replied philosophically. "It's the ambition, the lust for power, the wanting of something so badly you can taste it. You ache inside because you don't have it. That's the problem, and no amount of legalistic reform is ever going to change it.

"Look at the main congressional sponsor of the gift ban, Texas Rep. John Bryant. When he was asked by a reporter why he let three big-time lobbyists send a fundraising letter for him, he replied, 'They're not gifts. They're campaign contributions. There's a big difference.' Difference? You think the public sees any kind of difference? These people are crazy, all of them. That's the kind of appetite I'm talking about."

• • • •

I SPOKE with Roadtrip right after New Year's 1996.

"The beat goes on," he reported. "Just look around you. Rep. Alcee Hastings [D-Fla.] put his lawyer buddy Patricia Williams—to whom he owes more than five hundred grand in legal fees—on his congressional payroll. Ted Kennedy's wife is in the middle of a scholarship scandal in New Orleans. The so-called public interest groups are running with public money.

"And that's just another day in our town."

CHAPTER TEN

EGGHEADS AND QUOTE MACHINES

Dr. Thomas Mann asserts that today's lawmakers are more ethical, more knowl-edgeable about issues, more attentive to constituents and generally of a higher cal-iber than congressional members of a generation ago. Moreover, Mann and [Dr. Norman] Ornstein reject the notion—advanced by some congressional critics and a large segment of the public—that the only meaningful reform measures are bold strokes such as term limits, cutting congressional perks and salaries, slashing staff and outlawing the influence of special interests.

—Kevin Merida, *Washington Post*, 28 June 1993

The advantage Ron brings to me in the Washington PAC scene is that much of his income is dependent upon his relationship with me. He has got a vested interest in my staying in office.

—From Senator Bob Packwood's diary on 8 October 1991, on the usefulness of friendly lobbyist Ron Crawford

SEVEN FORTY-EIGHT A.M. is normally too early for morn-ing tea and much too early to come up with something clever to say to the Rev. Jesse Jackson on the way to the studio. It is defi-nitely too early to get ambushed on national television by an eminent Washington egghead.

But there I was, barely awake but live and in color on Wash-ington's *Fox Morning News* one fine spring morning in 1993. I was there to hawk my book, *Hill Rat*, which dealt with life behind the scenes on Capitol Hill. When I had done my spiel and the host turned to Dr. Thomas Mann, a political sci-entist at the prestigious Brookings Institute, I relaxed. This was

Washington at the height of the furor over the House banking scandal when the career of even the old bulls were falling like the dried-out cherry blossoms ringing the Tidal Basin. I figured that if anyone could corroborate my portrait of the seamier side of life in Washington, it was Mann.

I could not have been more wrong.

"I have no doubts about John's intentions," Mann intoned before going on to state that, in his opinion, my book contained "many small truths," but that despite these crumbs, my book added up to "the big lie: that members of Congress and Congress as an institution are interested only in appearances, in the individual reelection prospects of the members," and that the institution is "dominated by special interests" and that "it's all a fraud and a game." In short, Mann painted a pretty rosy picture of Congress.

I was stunned. Had Mann forgotten the smelly fall of the House of Wright and Tony Coelho only three years earlier? Was the checking scandal in the House a matter of no consequence? And was not the town awash (as always) in the campaign contributions of those who sought to buy influence?

After working as a flack and fundraiser for three Democratic members of Congress (including the inglorious post of consigliere for Jim Wright), I had a sufficiently jaundiced eye to find bizarre the assertion, by a prominent political scientist, that Congress is not ruled by special interests.

When I recounted the incident to one of my low friends in high places, he was appropriately unsympathetic toward my innocence. "Of course Mann knows the score," he snorted. "But did *you* know that Lee Hamilton [chairman of the House Foreign Affairs Committee] had enlisted Mann to work with the Joint Committee on the Reorganization of Congress?" Suddenly, the studio ambush made perfect sense.

The Joint Committee was supposed to be *the* institutional vehicle by which Congress would reform itself. Within policy circles, it has a high profile and was especially respected because of the caliber of people like Mann who had been tapped to participate. Hamilton, one of the staunchest defenders of the status quo on Capitol Hill, had just handed Mann the sort of plum assignment that comes around perhaps once in decade: it was the classic Washington conflict of interest, all the more corrupt in that the participants regarded it as a smashing success. Significantly, members serving on the Joint Committee had as a group raked in over $10 million in PAC campaign contributions. Like any streetwise Washington power player, Mann knew better than to bite the hand that fed him.

Throughout a period when the public's opinion of Congress continued to stand at a historic low, Mann continued his cheerleading for the institution. In the spring of 1994, for example, an article by Mann and Norman Ornstein that appeared in the *Brookings Review* painted a complacent picture of a Congress in minimal need of reform:

> [T]he deep and sustained public unhappiness with the performance of the institution and with its individual and institutional lapses fuels a demand for change.... [T]he sense of most members that they need to get their own house in order is palpable.
>
> [T]he lack of public confidence in Congress's ability to regulate and police itself... the past 15 years have seen an explosion of public scandals involving members of Congress... but the result is supremely ironic.... [T]he ethical tenor of congressional life has actually never been higher....

"Now let me get this straight," Roadtrip, also unsympathetic to my innocence, said when I described these events to him. "The members do Mann a favor. Mann pimps for them on television and in his final report. Mann keeps up the flackery, and they continue to give him access."

"That's right."

"So what's the problem? That's the way this town works."

After my book tour, I went home to the Pacific Northwest, where I received a congratulatory letter from a professor at Auburn University. He wrote to inform me that *Hill Rat* bolstered a theory of human motivation known as "public choice." According to this theory, people place their own self-interest, particularly in the field of economics, at the top of their list of priorities. Got that? Well, simple as this proposition may sound to anybody who's ever tried to get a driver's license in Washington (much less anybody who's ever contemplated the intricacies of a budget battle), it is a dangerously heretical notion for most traditional political scientists.

And political scientists are everywhere nowadays. You see them cajoling Congress, tarting up news stories with their pithy one-liners, or reading the entrails of the body politic on C-SPAN. They churn out op-ed pieces by the truckload. One editorial page editor I know recently lamented to me that he receives dozens of such articles a week—each author bent on self-promotion. Compounding the problem, Washington journalists generally have a Rolodex of pet eggheads to whom they can turn for a quote on just about anything—and at a moment's notice.

Given the blandishments of the quote circuit, it should come as no surprise that all too many political scientists forsake stringent analysis in favor of high visibility. In addition, many political scientists ignore the most obvious of issues, preferring instead to study some facet of an arcane world of their own imagining instead of the real, nitty-gritty world of politics. They are not at ease with the human factor.

This is a serious dereliction of duty. Thomas Kuhn wrote more than thirty years ago in *The Structure of Scientific Revolutions* that scientists are motivated as much by ambition as are other mortals. This is true for political scientists, too. Unfortunately, things are getting worse instead of better on this front.

"Look, I know I'm not the biggest fan of the eggheads," commented Roadtrip, who prides himself on the amount of political dirt under his fingernails. "But you have to hand it to them—they do their job well. They're our biggest and best front men for the media. It's not like they affect voter behavior or deliver states, but whenever the long knives are out for us, by the goddamn liberal goddamn reformers and public fucking interest groups, they make nice-nice. They're the best apologists you could ever hope for. We love 'em dearly."

In addition to being love objects for Roadtrip and his tribe, political scientists play a crucial supporting role in the Fall of Politics by providing the critical intellectual and academic underpinning for the notion of government as salvation for society's ills. Their impressive-sounding studies do more than simply serve up statistics and political interpretations, however. In the eyes of the broad public, political scientists bless the political culture. They decide what's worthy of scrutiny, and since political science pays homage to big government, the discipline helps to legitimize the entire political culture of Washington—and that includes Bill Clinton's vision of big government as the solution to our national woes. (Sure, from time to time Bill gets on a high horse and renounces "big government." But who's he fooling? Nobody but the *Washington Post*.)

When a political scientist of the stature of Thomas Mann says that Congress is not corrupt and is not dominated by special interests, people listen. They aren't always fooled but they do listen. It is of special note that the image of Congress that Mann says is not accurate—as corrupt, riddled by special interests, and interested only in its own reelection—is composed of precisely those seamy, real life things his discipline refuses (or is unable) to study. Some of the most visible—and obvious—issues don't get studied at all. For example, no political scientist came up with a model of negative ad campaigns until 1995.

This was late in the day, considering that the outcry over negative campaigning (and the related issue of the deterioration of public discourse) had begun in earnest with Lyndon Johnson's famous atomic cloud advertisement and continued with George Bush's Willie Horton or, for that matter, with Bill Clinton's class warfare. According to the two political scientists who developed the 1995 model, Drs. Sergio Skaperdas and Bernard Grofman of the University of California–Irvine, "Negative advertising is an important aspect of campaign competition but plays little or no role in existing [political scientists'] models of campaigns."

Not surprisingly, political science does have its critics. *Tikkun* editor and one-time Hillary guru Michael Lerner, for example, is an outspoken critic. Lerner finds political science "far away from the needs of human beings." Another critic, Charles Cook, an independent political analyst, has opined that "ninety-nine and one-half percent of the political scientists in this country have no idea how government works." And Neil Cote, a Florida newspaper columnist has said, "I've always thought the term 'political scientist' was an oxymoron—like jumbo shrimp or safe sex."

On a more serious note, Curtis Gans, director of the Committee for the Study of the American Electorate, put it more diplomatically: "I am lukewarm about the profession. There are many exceptions, but too often the techniques tend to quantify minutiae. Political science alone can't describe reality—you have to have some understanding."

What sparks this kind of derision normally reserved for American Football Conference teams in the Super Bowl?

First, as they say in the business, let's get a quick baseline. Just what is political science, and what is it supposed to do?

As befitting a self-anointed priesthood, political scientists profess lofty goals. Dr. Ted Lowi of Cornell, a former president of the American Political Science Association, said in an interview that "the purpose of political science is based on a great American tradition: if you do enough research on a topic, you can find an answer."

Often this answer involved—surprise, surprise!—government. In pure Clintonthink, for example, Lowi saw political science as walking hand-in-hand with an inherently activist government when he argued that "[w]e should do a lot of civic research, then propose government should get involved." As Lowi sees it, political science itself is part of the political phenomenon: "We exist to study politics, but we are products of it at the same time." Reflecting a common view of the profession, he viewed government as a neutral entity believing that through research, "we could solve social problems without ideology." He depicted a discipline that worked closely with government as they grew together, first in the reform spirit of the FDR administration, then with Congress and the New Deal ("we used research to help Congress come up with wise legislation"). Samuel Popkin of the University of California–San Diego and author of *The Reasoning Voter*, would concur: he has said political science's goal is "to find long-range answers to politics and government." (Popkin's self-described specialties: "peasants in small wars and American voters.")

Political science used to be a liberal preserve. Through the '50s and '60s, Lowi said, the dominant political scientist was liberal in the New Deal sense of being "practical and reformist, very comfortable with the New Deal and how to improve it." But now we have political scientists on both sides of the aisle. Lowi pointed to the resurgence of the Republican Party, which for the first time is more attuned to intellectual currents, resulting in the driving force behind the rise of the Heritage Foundation and the American Enterprise Institute. Work done at such institutions has had a profound effect on intellectual life, including the resurgence of classical economics.

So what exactly is political science? A representative answer came from Dr. Britano of the American Political Science Association. "Some would answer in a technical, scientific way, a narrow-science answer—the scientific method and its commitment to replication, evidence, controlling for causes," Britano said. "I would give a more general argument—scholarly work and a range of methods in science and the humanities."

What do these people who call themselves political scientists do all day? I had to know. A trip to the library was in order.

I decided to check the literature of the field. On my reading list were journals with enticing names like *American Political Science Review, Polity, Perspectives on Political Science, Legislative Studies Quarterly, Journal of Politics, American Journal of Political Science, Western Political Science Quarterly, Political Science and Politics, Political Analysis,* and the *Review of Politics.* My methodology was quite high-tech and scientific: see which articles from this supposedly liberal-leaning profession dealt with women, African Americans, health, and the rest of the liberal litany of interest-group politics. Then I added them up.

Why look at journal articles? They are the spawning ground of the profession, the legitimizer of future major work in the field, including books. Journal articles tell you what political scientists think is important, offering a snapshot of their priorities. They are the "indicator of what dominant research paradigm is coming through," according to American University professor James Thurber.

"That means what any egghead gives a shit about," Datahead explained, who, like most people who actually participate in politics, was contemptuous of the discipline's pretensions.

Of course, scholarly journals are not for the layman. Perish the thought! Dr. Nelson Polsby at Berkeley insists that "scholarly journals are for the promotion of communication among scholars" and not for consumption by us regular folks—

which is an even better reason to study the profession's crib notes. Polsby went on to admit, however, that the journals represent "a running record of what's on researchers' minds.... Political science gets its agenda from the progress of the discipline and the newspapers. They reflect the underlying political commitments."

Still, refusing to be intimidated, I took to the library.

My personal analysis and topical survey (decidedly unscientific, of course) of many of the major political science journals and media coverage from 1990–93 indicates a few recurring themes of their own:

A refusal to elevate major issues today to major priorities of the discipline, most notably issues affecting women and minorities. People with AIDS/HIV do not exist nor do women with breast cancer. African Americans are studied only in the wake of a crisis such as the South-Central L.A. riots. Before the riots, political science was seemingly unaware that the African American community and the LAPD were on a collision course.

With a few exceptions, such as Gary Jacobsen's examination of the political fallout of the House checking scandal, I found a decided reluctance on the part of political scientists to study Washington's inside political culture, especially its often tawdry human dimension. Even in the aftermath of Chappaquiddick, the Clarence Thomas confirmation hearings, and several years' worth of coverage of the Senator Bob Packwood scandal, I still couldn't find a single article on how women were treated by Washington's political culture.

Despite my low opinion of political scientists, I was dumbfounded when I actually discovered how badly women's issues were treated in the professional journals. For all the attention the media had lavished on Anita Hill in the Hill-Thomas debacle, the journals remained silent on the subject of women in Washington's unique culture. The voices of the female witnesses who had supported Thomas, less surprisingly, had not only been marginalized in the media but they had also been totally ignored in the field of political science. And 1992 was possibly even more explosive, with the Gennifer Flowers episode during the New Hampshire presidential primary; the decision of Senator Brock Adams (D-Wash.) to drop plans for reelection because of sexual harassment allegations; the primary loss of Illinois Rep. Gus Savage in part because of alleged abuse of a female Peace Corps worker in Africa; and, of course, the never ending saga of Bob Packwood, who that year faced more than a dozen allegations of sexual harassment that he was able to keep under wraps until after his narrow reelection victory. Even today, in the wake of disgraced Senator Bob Packwood's resignation, the issue of women within the political culture is not a high priority in the political science journals.

This isn't to say that you can't find articles about women. Indeed, you can find plenty of stuff on women's issues in the abstract (all within the context of the cultural left, of course)—day care, parental leave, "deconstructing the gender _____ (fill in the blank with your favorite anti-Western topic)." In fact, the list of articles reads like program notes at a NOW convention.

But where are the studies that illuminate the real lives of women: the specialized monographs, and the piles of statistic-laden reports that show that such a matter is an overriding priority of study? Where was political science—Dr. Thurber's "the study of what is and what ought to be"—as women faced new challenges?

Taking a walk, that's where. The reality of political science was a far cry from the rhetoric of "what is and what ought to be." Especially when it came to women. In 1992, the *Review of Politics* had one article about women—and none in 1991. *Legislative Studies Quarterly* had five, none of which dealt with the human dimension of women in political life. Out of the eleven major journals from 1990 to 1993, only one publication—*Political Science and Politics*—published a single article on sexual harassment, and that was in June 1991.

In addition, women's issues, especially breast cancer, don't merit study by political scientists, either. As different at-risk groups of people realize the connection between resources and advances in treatments, the politics of allocation will become acute and personal. Despite which, only one journal, *The Journal of Politics*, carried a single article on "distributive justice" and the politics of heath care. When the best analysis of the politics of breast cancer comes from *Ms.* magazine instead of MIT, something is amiss.

Other surprises?

The politics of the environment? One article.

Not a single article appeared on the politics of AIDS from any perspective—liberal, conservative, homosexual, heterosexual—nothing.

Same with anything having to do with gays and lesbians, in or out of closets or uniforms.

Ditto children's issues. And family values, the capstone of the 1994 election season? You'll have better luck at Wal-Mart.

Keep looking at almost every major issue with a strictly human dimension, and you'll see the same thing. (Are you catching on yet?)

The tidal wave of fundamental Christianity, the return of the baby-boomers to church, the first time there were more Manhattan yuppies in church than there were apparition sightings of the Virgin in South Texas? Five. Religion in electoral politics apparently doesn't interest the priesthood of political science.

You'll also find next to nothing on scandals in general, corruption, and influence peddling. What we know about these driving forces simply doesn't come from political scientists. Mann, for instance, has never bothered to study scandal or corruption in the political process, despite his many long years of analyzing Washington politics. Here is an astonishing spectacle: a congressional scholar who has never examined the corrupting influence of money—not the Keating Five, not the $5 billion savings and loan scandal, not Whitewater, not Bob Packwood—nothing. You'll find little if any attempt to understand working-class people or families, whose shift to cultural conservatism (and the subsequent political implications) took political science by surprise.

"The major burning issues have been ignored, especially with women and African Americans," argues University of Maryland professor Linda Williams. She sees this refusal to address contemporary issues as nothing new. "In the late 1960s, for example, no political scientist could tell you anything about the riots." Part of the problem, Williams said, is funding. "To some extent, the political scientists who bring in the big grants are at the top of their profession, and there is some unwillingness to fund those issues. It is difficult to find funding to do studies in domestic politics, such as an oversample of minorities or women."

While political scientists studied arcana of dubious relevance, outsider Michael Lerner, who spent ten years as a psychotherapist for working people and who is contemptuous of traditional political science, explained why blue-collar America moved to the right.

"You could miss everything if you stuck to economic issues," he explained. "Working people had a deep hunger for connection and respect, a deep hunger for some kind of community. Very few political scientists have any framework for these needs, and they miss out very badly. All they could do when working people voted for Ronald Reagan was to talk about the Great Communicator, claim that voters were manipulated because they were dumb, racist, or sexist. They couldn't imagine that there were some needs the right was speaking to that they couldn't measure."

Despite his occasional and annoying New Age leanings, Lerner, who bears quoting at some length, is always better than the political scientists when the human factor is involved. "Human beings have psychological, ethical, and spiritual needs that transcend the normal liberal agenda," Lerner wrote. "Liberals have tended to focus exclusively on economic entitlements and political rights.... It was the right, not the left, that recognized the crisis of meaning and went about creating a new politics of meaning.... What the right recognized, but the left would not, was that the society was in a deep ethical and spiritual crisis. And that crisis had everything to do with how the society and government are organized. The right understood it was impossible for individual families or churches to withstand the heavy assault on the values they were trying to teach their children." The right had severe flaws, Lerner believed, but "[n]evertheless, most people felt grateful to the right—because people intuitively understood that their children's rejection of ethically and spiritually sensitive values had something to do with outside influences." Lerner criticized the left because "the Democrats and the left simply had no understanding of the crisis of meaning whatsoever. Ethical and spiritual issues? For the liberals, these were purely personal, to be dealt with through psychotherapy or Sunday-only religion.... [T]he Democrats buried their heads in the sand, imagining that if they offered another middle-class entitlement or more highway construction they would win back the American people."

"You could miss everything if you stuck to economic issues. Working people had a deep hunger for connection and respect, a deep hunger for some kind of community. Very few political scientists have any framework for these needs," Lerner concluded.

Even political scientists are beginning to sense something is wrong with their discipline. Outgoing American Political Science Association president Ted Lowi unleashed a firestorm in the spring of 1992 when he offered a candid assessment of how the political science industry had ended up in such a fix. Lowi wagged his finger at his colleagues and admonished them with three central criticisms. First, political science is a product of the state, and they ought to own up to that. Second, there are several political sciences and they are the product of what is studied. And third, there were reasons "other than the search for the truth" for what political science does. It is important to note, Lowi argued, that the discipline could not exist without the modern bureaucratic state. And the dominance of public opinion analysis, he added, is "a product of its compatibility with bureaucratic thought-ways, rather than the result of successful discourse within political science."

Lowi blasted the sterile world of political science journals for their absence of passion. "Too few of the articles seek to transcend their analysis to join a more inclusive level of discourse. There is consequently little substantive controversy." At the end of the address, Lowi zeroed in on his primary target: "Political scientists of the Left, Right, and center are a unity in their failure to maintain a clear and critical consciousness of political consciousness…. At the end of my pilgrimage, I have come to the conclusion that among the sins of omission of modern political science, the greatest of all has been the omission of passion."

Passion? You can read the scholar-to-scholar texts of the discipline and dance through an intellectual la-la land, finding no inkling that popular fury against government and the culture of government would produce fourteen out of fourteen ballot referenda victories for term limits, that H. Ross Perot could win the votes of nineteen million Americans, that the sexual proclivities of presidential candidate Bill Clinton could add an unparalleled dimension to the dynamics of presidential elections, even that George Bush could lose….

Despite Ted Lowi's contention that "our research agenda is

set by what we see on the front page," there remains an over-whelming preference for the statistical ("Accountability and U.S. Senate Elections: A Multivariate Analysis"), the procedural ("A Theory of Voting Equilibria"), and the *au courant* ("Hidden Desires and Missing Persons: A Feminist Deconstruction of Foucault").

Political scientists have developed a dizzying array of mathematical models, voting studies, and the role of parties, conventions, and constitutions. While these subjects are no doubt interesting to *someone*, they nevertheless represent a sort of leechcraft by which the body politic is sucked dry of any human element.

"There has been a gradual increase in the weight given to science as the paradigm of knowledge," Lerner explained. "To them, reality is only really real when it's repeatable and observable in the physical world that can be measured. Political science as a 'science' is the outcome of this general trend—to develop laws of political behavior that are repeatable and observable." Unfortunately, as Lerner points out, "you get the quintessential error made by Marx—to have a science of politics that worked well only to the extent that people were dominated. The more freedom people have, the less political science has to offer. It always ends up predicting regular, conformist behavior."

This blind faith in scientific order can be, well, blinding. James Guth, who teaches at Furman University, has noted that religion, so important to so many ordinary people, doesn't interest the priesthood of politics. Guth has written that "the influence of religion in electoral politics has seldom excited much inquiry among mainstream political scientists and sociologists, whose secularism... [is] ignoring a poweful force."

"There is a real antipathy toward the world of lived experience," observed dissident political scientist Russell Dondero of Oregon's Pacific University, which deliberately names its department "Politics and Government," and pointedly not "Political Science." Dondero once took a sabbatical not to engage in arcane research, but to actually observe the real world of politics as a lobbyist for hunger issues with the Oregon legislature.

Lerner concurs. "Political scientists cannot understand what actually motivates people in politics. Their rigid categories never capture the flow of meaning."

"You have three cultures within the political science community," Dondero added. "One, the elegant, theoretical constructs of the behavioralists; two, the deconstructionists; and three, those who use their skills to sell themselves to the establishment and become part of the punditry as well."

Dondero points out that the profession's preoccupation with being a "science" is an American phenomenon. "The empiricists lost the battle in Canada and Europe, which stress the importance of cultural and intellectual history. But science is God in this culture, and political scientists coming out of World War II realized that power."

The preference for statistics and theorems over lived experience extends, of all places, to Washington politics. You'd think there couldn't be a better window in America to study the human factor in politics, but most political science analysis coming from Washington ignores any "live body" approaches:

Poli. Sci. 101: Try this test.

Here's a simple pop quiz to determine the level of your awareness of political science today.

Question: Which one of the following is a political science journal article from the '90s?

A. "Theft in Office," analyzing former House Postmaster Robert Rota's 19 July 1993 guilty plea to embezzlement in the House Post Office probe and government documents indicating he helped former House Ways and Means Committee Chairman Dan Rostenkowski steal $21,300.

B. "Abuse of Power by Speakers of the House," from former House Speaker Jim Wright's shady book deals, defeated House Speaker Tom Foley's insider sweetheart stock issue transactions, to current Speaker Newt Gingrich.

C. "Women on Capitol Hill: Different Strokes," including sexual harassment issues ranging from the Clarence Thomas–Anita Hill hearings to current allegations involving Senator Bob Packwood; also including how Paula Corbin Jones was treated by national womens' organizations in the aftermath of her sexual harassment lawsuit against Bill Clinton.

D. "Estimation Across Data Sets: Two-Stage Auxiliary Instrumental Variable Estimation," which develops the 2SAIV estimator, proves its consistency, and derives its asymptotic variance.

If you picked D, go to the head of the class.

Here are two recent incidents that show why political science is so divorced from the politics it studies.

The first was "Regulating Lobbyists and Interest Group Influence," a February 1993 article by the University of Georgia's Dr. Scott Ainsworth in the *Journal of Politics*.

Ainsworth used a "game theoretical model" with complex equations to try to figure out how lobbyists and members of Congress communicated.

This was one of his equations:

$$\mu\,(t^{*}\,|\,s') = [d(s'\,|\,t^{*})p(t^{*})]/[\Sigma_{\,(t\,|\,\Omega)}[d(s'\,|\,t)p(t)]]$$

One of his conclusions: "Lobbyists are not harmless, but they can be controlled."

That's not a bad place to start, and for a political scientist today, an excellent one because it admits there are people in the political universe. He had another good premise, too: "the problem, quite simply, is that it is impossible to determine precisely whom an interest group represents." When I asked him what had been the reaction of the members of Congress and lobbyists studied, he said most of the article's content had come from secondary sources. Ainsworth admitted he had not interviewed a single lobbyist or member of Congress for his study about lobbying and interest group influence.

Ainsworth had employed a "game theory" approach, and I asked him about it. He said, "It's more intuitive than the presentation would let on. The reason to make fancy models is to test our intuition. You perform straightforward statistical analysis to test hunches.

"We select strategies, independent of one another," he explained, "and the communication comes in when I say something, you say something—is that signal indicative of something else?"

"If only it were that easy," a K Street warrior sighed. "If only they *stayed* rented—my life would be so much easier. Every typical day begins with some member we gave a ton of money to and now he's fucking us."

And the equation? I asked.

"I think I saw it in Hillary's health care bill."

CHAPTER ELEVEN

ANNOYING MAN

ENTER DR. NORMAN ORNSTEIN, the King of Prof Quote.

Dr. Ornstein could exist only in Washington. He came out of congressional scholarship to the American Enterprise Institute, a think tank that rose to prominence during the Reagan administration. Ornstein's official title is "resident scholar and political analyst," but his real job is self-promotion. His relentlessness has become a Washington legend. The *National Journal* once had a poster of Ornstein in the newsroom with the international red circle through it, so reporters would not quote him as automatically as they had been doing.

He is a politician without office, but not without portfolio. There are times when Norm, as he is universally called in Washington, is everywhere, from the *MacNeil-Lehrer Newshour* on PBS to the opinion pages of the *Washington Post*. He has his own opinion column in *Roll Call*, the insider's newspaper of Congress. He has another regular gig on *USA Today*, which gives him access to virtually every community in the country. Norman Ornstein is almost singlehandedly responsible for the invention of the news media term "prof quote." Most political news stories are structured the same these days: you have the lead, supporting developments, some background, then the slot for "expert opinion." That's where many reporters stick in a quote from their favorite political scientist to give their favorite point the blessing of scholarship. Norm is all too often the pundit of choice.

"If I could only give good Norm," one political scientist told me, "I'd be a millionaire."

That's because Norm delivers.

Norm is part of a growing number of political scientists who have turned into racetrack handicappers and palace eunuchs; they have discovered that rubbing shoulders with the powerful is a lot more rewarding than taking them on. His is a political analysis of a mannered age—not unlike pre-Revolutionary France, where the aristocracy kept clever houseguests from the lower classes who had to eat in the kitchen with the help but who were summoned on occasion to the main dining room to produce laudatory literature, or make the dukes laugh. Norm is a one-man Milli Vanilli who lip-synchs the political culture's message that nothing is fundamentally wrong with the status quo.

Not surprisingly, his fans are legion. Berkeley's Nelson Polsby has called him "absolutely first-rate. His standing among academic specialists on Congress is high." Political analyst Charles Cook wished "there were two hundred more like him." "What makes [him] successful is that [he] can take complex issues and explain them in understandable words, without dumbing it down too far," Cook said. He said he found an enormous amount of jealousy in academia, particularly for the kind of money Ornstein makes.

I am not one of Ornstein's fans.

Giving good Norm smacks of being the home team's paid sportscaster or racetrack handicapper. His articles are carefully crafted to curry favor. He will mention or offer limited mainstream criticism, but he will never challenge Washington's political culture directly. In fact, Norm sees himself so much a part of that culture that he uses the royal "we" when discussing congressional developments on PBS. During the 1994 health care reform debate, for example, Norm said on PBS that "chances are *we're* going to be doing that… and *we* have not yet devised a process… then *we've* got to go to conference committee… and that's what *we're* maneuvering toward here… " (emphasis added).

Norm frequently has a kind word for those in power. White House aide Roy Neel is a "savvy veteran." (Savvy enough to cash in on his connections and add his name to the list of political hacks who have moved from the Clinton White House to well-paid positions in Washington's political culture.) George Stephanopoulos (whom Norm likes) has "prodigious talents." Ross Perot (whom Norm doesn't like) is "self-appointed." Dan Rostenkowski is "that master negotiator."

Norm does not take political chances and does not threaten Washington's culture of influence or its favored players. In his opening analysis of the new Congress on 9 January 1995, he never once mentioned the need to clean up the political system. Norm loves a good piling-on, but won't take a swing on his own. He will criticize the Congressional Black Caucus, but he never laid a glove on former Speaker Tom Foley.

Although he does not cite scholarly research from his field to back up his views, he promotes his own congressional testimony and related writings heavily. In fact, the inherent caution and scholarly conservatism of political science—one of the discipline's attributes—is antithetical to his activities. And with the exception of polling, he does not comment on the products of his own profession.

For the practitioner of a discipline that prides itself on the accumulation of knowledge, Norman rarely quotes any other political scientist, competing or otherwise.

He *is* very much on top of the hot topic of the moment, regardless of whether he has the personal academic expertise and scholarly research to back it up. If there's a headline, you can be sure Norm has an opinion, and that he's faxed it around town. He does not break new ground. Norm's place is a Congress of mechanics and procedures where the action takes place in a graduate school seminar—there are no emotions, no ambition, no money, no deals, no betrayals. His specialty is play-by-play announcing of political housekeeping—schedules, timetables, coalitions, and voting blocs.

A NEXUS computer search of his byline articles and commentary in the '90s reveals four recurring themes:

- He regularly makes wildly inaccurate predictions of future political developments—trust me, you don't want Norm as your stockbroker.
- He defends the status quo to the point of preposterousness.
- He depicts bloodless, depopulated politics, devoid of any human reality.
- He will talk about anything.

Let's deconstruct Norm one step at a time—in good scholarly fashion, of course.

Bad predictions. Here's a sampling:

November 26, 1993. While defending the Clinton administration's legislative record on PBS, Norm said, "… and movement toward completion—we're not quite there—but we'll almost certainly get there—of a whole series of reform packages, campaign finance reform, lobbying reform, and pretty major congressional reform. Those are all I'd say 85 to 90 percent of the way there."

Actual result: absolutely nothing happened, and none of the reform legislation passed.

May 27, 1994. On PBS again, discussing the Clinton administration's health care reform legislation, Norm predicted that "there is at least a 70 percent chance of its passage." Again, on 13 June: "Yes, Virginia, there is still likely to be a health care reform bill passed and enacted this year. I'd put [the odds] at about 60 percent."

Actual result: a total rout.

August 8, 1994. In his *Roll Call* column, Norm predicted that "1994 should be an election of minimal change in the House ... so the Democrats' losses in 1994 should be closer to the 12 lost by the GOP in 1968 than the 26 lost by the GOP in 1982...." On 17 October 1994, in *Fortune* magazine, he gazed into his crystal ball and predicted that "this anti-Washington anger is probably not focused enough to sweep away longstanding Democratic majorities in the House and Senate."

Actual result: you already know. *that one.*

November 20, 1994. In the *Washington Post*, Norm trumpeted the birth of a new Republican middle that would brake the ambitions of House Speaker Newt Gingrich, Majority Leader Dick Armey, and the rest of the barbarians.

Actual result: no one has heard of the emerging middle since.

December 7, 1995. Ornstein criticized Oregon's election to replace U.S. Sen. Bob Packwood, the first-ever U.S. Senate race to be conducted by vote-by-mail, as one that "trivializes" the democratic process.

Actual result: 216,286 "more" voters participated in the primary elections than in 1994's nonpresidential primary.

Now if you found a member of Congress who had that poor political sense, you'd haul him before the Ethics Committee on charges of sheer stupidity. But if you're Norman Ornstein, your reputation only waxes because you've profited from the politician's rule: no one ever keeps track of your promises to the public.

In another area, Norm is consistent: he never misses the opportunity to attack reform, especially if it's from outside Washington's political culture. Throughout the 1994 election year, he mounted a jackhammer attack on all sources critical of Congress—the news media, reformers, and "Congress bashers." Norm's world is dominated by a shadowy anti-Congress conspiracy—no names, of course, and shhhh! they might be watching—just dark forces and a malevolent "them." In his writings, Norm fashions himself to be Congress's Horatius at the bridge, a fatherly figure of reason and moderation against all those hysterical people out there in the provinces.

He began his 1994 offensive on 14 February by adopting Bill and Hillary Clinton's technique of attacking the news media. "When it comes to reporting about Congress," Norm complained, "all the normal rules of fairness and scrupulousness go out the window; cheap shots are common and increasingly so for network news shows and newsmagazines...."

A week later, he attacked the concept of a constitutional amendment requiring a balanced budget, and in early April, he criticized Senate passage of a line-item veto for the president. On 11 April, he struck again, this time defending the Clintons on Whitewater by attacking the way the press handled its coverage.

In a remarkable performance, he hectored the *Washington Post* on its placement of Whitewater stories, defended Hillary Rodham Clinton's one-day, $100,000 commodity profits as "perfectly legal," and supported White House adviser George ("this conversation never happened") Stephanopoulos's attempt to interfere in the appointment of a Whitewater investigator. Norm finally attacked journalists for doing exactly what he does—raking in the cash from speaking fees.

"Norm ought to be on our payroll," a White House staffer told me. "The problem is that some people think he is. It's almost embarrassing. He goes so far overboard to kiss our asses that it becomes a problem—it's just too blatant. If he has any friends, they ought to tell him to cool it. He's going to get his legs cut out from under him when all this [Whitewater] stuff eventually comes out."

Subsequently, Norm changed targets and started to attack lobbying reform. In particular, Norm was against the banning of gifts to members of Congress by special interests. According to Ornstein, members of Congress would answer the following questions the same way he would:

> Are lawmakers bought by lunches and dinners paid for by lobbyists? The answer is no. Do their votes change because of gifts proffered by lobbyists, or golf and tennis junkets underwritten by them? No again.... Members have not developed friendships with lobbyists so that they can cadge free meals, receive lavish gifts, or take trips to nice places.

In an inexplicable leap of logic, Norm argued that banning gifts from lobbyists would "demean public service... gift reform is simply another step in the process of chipping away at every positive element of congressional life."

Norm went on to defend congressional junkets and free vacations:

> It also needs to be said that the overwhelming bulk of the charges made about Congress in the junket and speech business is hypocritical and unfair. Lawmakers do go to charity events and to association or corporation meetings, which are often, indeed usually, in nice places at beautiful resorts.
>
> Big deal. So do I.... We get something in return for giving up precious time taken away from other important responsibilities.

On 18 September 1994, with the midterm election campaign in full swing, Norm entered what Roadtrip called "his finest hour": an impassioned plea in the *Washington Post* that special-interest money has no impact on the legislative process. "Money has a very limited impact," Ornstein claimed. "Most members of Congress are not motivated primarily, or even significantly, by the desire for more money; nor do they trade votes for dollars, or let the agenda be set or dominated by lobby spending...."

"I felt like writing him a check," Roadtrip chuckled. "But then I thought no, it would be an insult, because whatever amount I wrote in wouldn't be enough for what he does for us. I was at a fundraising reception for a member and this Republican lobbyist comes up to me and says, Roadtrip, you see Norm's piece in the *Post* last Sunday? Yeah, I said, everybody's been laughing about it. Well, he says, pulling out a $1,000 check and waving it, what the fuck are we doing wasting our time here for? We both start laughing. He then goes up to the desk, drops off his check, talks to the member, and three days later he got his amendment."

While Norm takes a tolerant stance toward Congress, he's not above the odd personal attack. Ellen Miller at the Center for Responsive Politics, Joan Claybrook at Public Citizen, and Charles Lewis at the Center for Public Integrity are, according to Norm, guilty of inciting journalists to say mean things about PACs. As everybody knows, money is irrelevant on Capitol Hill:

> But apart from journalists and professional public-interest advocates [Norm being one as well], virtually all close observers of the legislative process believe money has a very limited impact.... In fact, there is an almost complete disconnect between academic findings and journalistic interpretations. Dozens of researchers have used the most sophisticated techniques to measure factors influencing congressional votes; all have found that [other factors] have stronger correlations to lawmakers' behavior than PAC contributions or other monies.

Incredibly, Norm went on to claim that "most members of Congress are not motivated primarily, or even significantly, by the desire for more money, nor do they trade votes for dollars, or let the agenda be set or dominated by lobby spending." (Homework assignment for Norm: the Packwood diaries.)

This was vintage Norm, and a refrain that he had begun, as early as 1992, proving once again that the old adage—the only thing louder than a politician squealing for credit is one who's running for cover—apparently holds true for their professional apologists as well. In the 14 July 1992, *USA Today*, for example, he deplored that "most Americans have been convinced that policymakers live by their own rules, insulated from the rest of us and corrupted by the process." In other articles, he has defended the operations of the House bank, pooh-poohed the running-up of House restaurant tabs, opposed term limits, and argued that too much money is not a problem in politics—all without citing a single research product of his own or from his discipline to back up his positions, which marched in lockstep with those of the discredited former House Democratic leadership.

The American people, of course, gave the Norm Ornsteins of Washington politics their own verdicts on Election Day 1994. But Norm went down swinging. As late as the last week of the campaign, he was still flailing at "Congress bashers" and shrieking that term limits, the line-item veto, and a balanced budget amendment wouldn't work. Like a crushed insect with limbs still thrashing, he blamed "the campaign of Congress-bashing" for undermining the legitimacy of Congress.

Norm has his quirks, too, the most amusing of which is his propensity to talk about anything under the sun, qualified or not:

- With a breathtaking view of his own abilities, he informed President-elect Clinton in an op-ed article on 2 November 1992 "how to turn the country around."
- He advocated restricting the sale of bullets and ammunition as a supplement to gun control.
- Straying even further from his field of research, he waded into the Medicare fight in June 1995 to warn Democrats not to try to take partisan advantage of the Republicans' problems.

On 26 April 1993, Norm wrote in *Roll Call* that federal prosecutors "must end their big-game hunt of politicians." He called for a prosecutorial hands-off of elected officials such as Illinois Rep. Dan Rostenkowski.

The reality was that Rosty had been the quintessential congressman for sale:

- According to *Congressional Quarterly*, nearly one-third of the $358,331 in operating expenses reported by Rostenkowski's campaign and his personal political action committee in 1990 and 1991 went for lifestyle or income—trips, golf, vacations, fancy restaurant tabs, and so on.
- Rostenkowski took eighty-two days of trips and vacations from special interest groups and charged his campaign and political action committee for $33,000 in dinners in 1990–91.
- Almost echoing Dr. Ornstein's words, Rostenkowski called the investigation a "fishing expedition and a political witch hunt."

On 20 July 1993, court documents and news accounts revealed that Robert Rota, the former House postmaster, had given sworn statements that he had helped Rostenkowski embezzle $21,300 and tens of thousands more for an undisclosed number of other House members. And on 31 May 1994, a federal grand jury indicted Rostenkowski for allegedly taking over $600,000 in public funds from congressional accounts over a twenty-year period and using the money to benefit himself and his cronies. The indictment also alleged that Rostenkowski obstructed justice by urging a witness to withhold evidence. "If Rostenkowski is ever tried by a jury of his peers, he should pray that Norm becomes the foreman," Roadtrip commented.

On one occasion, Norm coauthored an op-ed article with one of the capital's top lobbyist, Ken Duberstein, a former White House aide to President Bush and a symbol of the revolving-door syndrome between positions of public trust and opportunities for selling it. In an article entitled "Perspective on the 104th Congress" in the *Los Angeles Times* on 5 January 1995, Ornstein and Duberstein wrote:

> The real chance for governing will come in the second hundred days. At that point, there will be a long list of agenda items ripe for final action on a broad bipartisan basis, on the GATT model, health insurance reform, Superfund, safe drinking water, mining reform, telecommunications reform, crime bill revision, tort and product liability reform, lobbying and gift reform....

In the *Washington Representatives* directory, Duberstein's firm listed as among its clients Aetna Life and Casualty, the National Cable Television Association, Time Warner, Shell Oil, the Monsanto Corporation, Dow Corning, United Airlines, and others—all directly affected by one or more of the issues on which he and Norm were calling for action.

As Samuel Popkin put it, "The Norman Ornsteins of the world are at the wrong end of the telescope."

And here's how you can find out just exactly how wrong they are. In a scientific test on its World Wide Web page, *Below the Beltway* is going to track the predictions of Norm and his crew, and compare them with predictions received from the same issues and questions from the following:

■ a Ouija board,
■ the famous "Eight Ball" answer toy, and
■ the even-more famous Psychic Friends Network.

Yessireee, see how the political scientists fare against some real experts! It's all on *Below the Beltway*'s World Wide Web page at **http://www.teleport.com/~jackley/pundit.html**!

CHAPTER TWELVE

THE WEB

I don't believe there will be government left on this planet in 50 years. I don't think there will be a need for one. I actually wonder if there is a need for one right now. And I am not joking about this.

—John Perry Barlow, Internet advocate
Electronic Frontier Foundation

YEAH, YEAH, YEAH.
—Roadtrip's reaction to Barlow's comments while on his way to deliver more PAC checks to new Republican members of the House of Representatives' "reform" class of 1994

THERE IS ONE PLACE left in America that's not too afraid or too complacent to take on absolutely anything: the Internet.

"You're on your own here, bud," Roadtrip advised when I told him that the Internet was the next stop on the journey, and his comment didn't surprise me too much. Like many lobbyists and others in Washington's political culture, he likes doing things the way he was used to doing them, and part of that tradition is to eschew anything "technical." It was a kiss of political death in the '80s on Capitol Hill, for example, to be associated in any way with the computer services in a member's office—unless you were screaming at the top of your lungs that the goddamn machine had just eaten your floor statement ten minutes before a debate was to begin. If you were branded a "technical" person, however, you were unfit to analyze legislation, speak in staff meetings, or go drinking with the member. Drinking with the member is of course the most serious of these things and it generally took years of political or legislative apprenticeship to qualify.

With regard to computers, things have changed.

The Internet, a global network of 2.2 million computers in 135 countries, is undergoing explosive growth at an annual rate of 10 percent to 15 percent in the United States, depending on whose numbers you believe. According to an 11 September 1995 *Miami Herald* report, the Internet is expanding at an average rate of over 40 percent in most regions of the world. Germany's growth rate is 41 percent, and Japan's is 40 percent, while the Russian federation is speeding ahead at 68 percent for the first half of this year. The world's fastest growing nation, in Internet terms, is the Faroe Islands, which has an expansion rate of 99 percent in Internet domains. (Every time a sheepherder leaves the flocks to log on, their numbers double.) Here in the United States, a July 1995 national survey of Internet users by O'Reilly and Associates found that 34 percent were women and 43 percent had annual household incomes of $35,000 to $75,000. And an October 1995 sounding by the A.C. Nielson Company showed that about 24 million adults in the United States and Canada had used the Internet in the first three months. (Number junkies can find the entire study at **http:1/nww.commerce.net/**.)

Broadly defined, cyberspace is more than the Internet. According to one leading definition, cyberspace is a "bioelectronics environment that is literally universal: It exists everywhere there are telephone wires, coaxial cables, fiber-optic lines or electromagnetic waves. This environment is inhabited by knowledge, including incorrect ideas, existing in electronic form.... [T]he key is software, a special form of electronic knowledge that allows people to navigate through the environment and make its contents understandable to the human senses in the form of written language and sound."

In case you're not familiar with Internetese, there's a quick plate of terms that can carry you a long way, especially at Washington cocktail parties:

The Internet. The global system of interconnected computers.
The World Wide Web. Software that lets you publish on the Internet and view pictures, graphics, audio, and video, as well as access all kinds of data bases. The Web uses hypertext markup language (HTML) that allows you to link instantly with other Web pages all over the world.
Web Page. Magazine-like site on the Internet that is interactive, can be linked all over the world to other Web pages (also called Web sites), uses e-mail, and can provide words, pictures, audio, and video.
Browser. The program you use to view the Web, such as Netscape or Mosaic.
Links. Words or pictures on Web pages that, when you click on them, take you to other Web pages or data bases.
Hits. The number of times a Web page has been looked at.
URLs. Uniform resource locators. A fancy way of saying "Internet address."
Newsgroups. Sometimes called Usenet groups, these are areas on the Internet where anyone can post and read messages on the topic of the newsgroup. There are over 12,000 newsgroups on the Internet and growing.

Warning: "technical." The Internet is like everything else in Washington: if you sound like you know too much about it, you might be accused of being on a crusade. Stick to big-picture stuff like "implications," "changing world," and "stuff our kids do all the time in school that you and I will never understand." That is how to sound important.

Beyond the fruit and flowers promised by its prophets, the Net is fertile ground for opinion-making and opinion-expressing. Hundreds of new newsgroups appear each week, dedicated to every possible topic imaginable, from computers and sociology to hobbies, politics, sex, entertainment, sports, and more.

Rod Kuckro is one of the new breed of politically savvy Internet experts who have come out of Washington's journalistic and public affairs community. Kuckro was a Washington journalist for more than twenty years with Gannett News Service, the *Cincinnati Enquirer,* the *Oakland Tribune*, and McGraw-Hill, where he worked for most of the '80s covering energy, economic policy, and the White House. He also served as press secretary to my old boss, U.S. Rep. Thomas Luken (D-Ohio), and more respectably, he has also worked for U.S. Rep. Pete Stark. Today, Kuckro is editor-in-chief for one of Washington's most advanced electronic publishing firms, where he handles World Wide Web development.

"There's been a sea change in the way government makes information available to the public," Kuckro observed. "Yesterday, service bureaus were selling data. Today, full-text documents are on line, and by the end of next year, President Clinton has ordered all federal agencies to do electronic commerce. On the other side of the Mall, House Speaker Gingrich has brought Capitol Hill into the twentieth century. There used to only be a handful of members with access to the Internet before Gingrich. Now it's unusual *not* to be on the Net."

Kuckro noted that the number of Internet users, while relatively small compared to the population as a whole, are the very people policymakers and politicians want to reach the most—college-educated white males, 18–40, and clustered in the politically strong suburbs. "Women are largely absent as a major user group of this technology," he conceded. The Democrats, he added, can't communicate with their core constituencies as a whole on the Net because of demographic obstacles such as poverty, lower educational levels, and lack of access to the expensive technology.

Indeed, research suggests that, in general, the Net today is not Clinton-friendly. As the Silicon Media Web page notes, "Internet users fit a profile that is particularly favorable to conservative and moderate electronic political campaigns." According to a poll published in February 1995 in *Newsweek*, nearly half describe themselves as Republicans. Democrats and Independents, however, are running neck and neck on the Net—24 percent and 28 percent, respectively. The education level is slightly above average—about three-quarters of the Net population have at least some college, while some have advanced degrees.

Politics on the Net is not exactly your father's civics class, and it is definitely not the civics you learned in school. In keeping with the general tenor of life on the Net, politics on the Net is brawling, loud, and crass. On occasion, however, discourse on the Internet is thoughtful. It is, in short, not a bad reflection of American politics as a whole.

Think of the Net as a collective extension of our inner chaos. It is difficult to predict its ultimate impact on politics. But the advent of the Net will forever change the relationship between Washington and the rest of the country. The public's newfound ability to respond instantly to policymakers, coupled with the ability to disseminate information to millions in the twinkling of an eye, will have a twofold impact on politics: decentralization (which could increase calls for accountability) and more rumor-mongering.

"The ability to send rumors and conduct information warfare is tremendous," Dr. Mich Kabay, director of education at the National Computer Security Association, told me. "I warn politicians: you are going to see an increase in the amount of misinformation being sent out deliberately to spark rumors. It's too easy to pass up."

"In social psychology, one of the observations about how people form judgments about issues is that salience influences judgment," Kabay contended. "Until Internet access becomes more widespread, anyone sending e-mail to a congresscritter is likely to be considered with greater interest than someone sending snailmail—simply because of the novelty."

Dirty tricks are likely. "Congresscritters naturally weigh public comments with an eye to voter preferences," Kabay said. "How will the congressional staff judge how many people sent 20,000 messages [on any given issue] if there is no authentication of the identity of the senders? Without public key signatures, a computer program could generate thousands of e-mail messages using randomizers for the text and a list of fraudulent identifiers. Even with public keys, if the Bad Guys chose to certify thousands of their own pseudonyms, nobody could stop them—and it is unlikely that Congresscritters would know which keys had been certified by criminals."

"Anyone can send e-mail with a fake name. America Online and CompuServe have no validation of a person's name," Kabay continued. "And the commercial providers make no attempt to validate the identities of their users. Furthermore, it is difficult or impossible to trace back a message, which means it would be easy for an organized campaign to distort the political process. If a politician sets up a mailbox on the Net, he or she would be foolish to accept raw input at face value."

"The problem in cyberspace is that once information enters it, it's impossible to eradicate," he explained. "The Internet has no mechanisms for tracking messages, and any retraction or rebuttal doesn't know where to go."

The Web is the most important segment of the Internet for political applications. It is an all-in-one communications site that can be instantly interactive. Unlike the anonymous participants in commercial service chat rooms and the Usenet groups, you generally know to whom you're talking. If you've ever watched the names hurled back and forth in cyberspace in the anonymous groups, this feature will be welcome. There is also variety. You can turn to the Democratic Congressional Campaign Committee's site, the Clinton White House, Ross Perot's United We Stand America, or Pat Buchanan's presidential campaign site. The graphics, images, and ability to link instantly anywhere allows the Web to give you a tidal wave of information.

The Web is evolving so rapidly that nobody knows what its ultimate effect on politics will be. At the August 1995 "Aspen Summit: Cyberspace and the American Dream II," Jeffrey Eisenach, Newt Gingrich's technology adviser, told the press, "What has happened is, a whole new group of issues and shared interests has arisen and now dominates the discussion. It's not that the people talk to each other through the Internet and that reduces conflict. In fact, there is lots of evidence that conflict is as great as ever before."

As you might guess, the Aspen Summit is available on the Internet (at **http://www.townhall.co/pff**). "Welcome to the Progress and Freedom Foundation WWW Homepage," the title bar proclaimed. (The Aspen Institute continues to live on in cyberspace. According to Eisenach, it received 6,500 hits the Monday after the Summit alone.)

The Aspen Web site is well constructed. The graphics are clean and sober and simple (this could be a first for the Web). The opening page fits on a single screen and directs you to various publications, personnel, or the Aspen Summit. A simple click on the summit icon takes you directly to the vision statement (which is mercifully short). The discussion is set up to continue through 1996, focusing on the "role of government" and other topics.

Another site is **http://aspen.ppf.org/help/forums.html**; you simply follow the instructions and plunge right in. The beauty of discourse on the Net is that you have equal standing with big-name people. For instance, Rep. Vin Weber and Senators Tom Daschle, Richard Lugar, and Larry Pressler are known users.

Roadtrip, however, remained dubious. "I told you that you were on your own because I'm still not that familiar with the Net, but you'd better take a closer look," Roadtrip chuckled when I told him some more about the new on-line political world. "But I'll bet our crowd's already beat you to it."

He was right. In politics there's one thing of which you can be certain: wherever there's action, you'll find the lobbyists and consultants. Where there's any way to schlep their schlock, they'll do it. It's already happening. At one end of the spectrum is the new firm (they're all new in this business), Green Lake in Michigan, which put out a 1995 Internet press release titled "Information Superhighway Paves the Campaign Trail—Green Lake Introduces Campaigns to the Internet." (Actually, Green Lake was not the first pioneer of campaigning on the Internet; others had been there long before.)

"In campaign '96 there will be those who blaze the trail to victory by using the latest technology to get their message across," claimed Green Lake founder Lynn Hostetter. "What candidates have on the Internet is a potentially large untapped voter base. Internet communications can be designed to give constituents and voters a much more personalized campaign message." Green Lake is the boutique of the Internet personalized service, offering a small client list, and an indifference to whether the candidate is a Democrat or Republican.

By contrast, Marlowe and Company ("Your Washington Lobbyist Connection on the Net" at **http://www.cais.com/marlowe/**) is the Neiman-Marcus of the Net.

The company is refreshingly up front about the business of Washington. "Every day, Congress and the executive branch make decisions that affect each of us," their Web site says. "They result from pressures that government feel from a variety of competing interests. Marlowe and Company is an experienced public affairs consulting firm that can help you influence the outcome of a congressional or executive branch policy decision." Marlowe "knows who the key players are.... Our contacts provide us with the inside information we need to help you stay ahead of developments, and our expertise enables us to create strategies that help you get what you want from Washington."

"Existing computer data bases are not sufficiently customized to meet the diverse needs of lobbyists," Howard Marlowe said. "That is why Marlowe and Company developed its own propriety data base system: POWERNET." According to Marlowe, this system takes information about members of Congress, their districts, political history, and voting records and combines it with PAC contributions, vote ratings, key contacts, and so on. "We use this customized analysis to determine which members of Congress to target for lobbying grassroots mobilization, and cosponsorship effort."

Marlowe has both technology and contacts. Howard Marlowe is a veteran of twenty-five years on the Hill as associate director of legislation for the AFL-CIO, and two consecutive terms as president of the American League of Lobbyists (yes, Virginia, they even have their own trade association). His client list includes the American Public Gas Association, the railroad engineers union, the textile workers union, the Edison Electric Institute, and various airports and municipalities.

"Listen to this," I told Roadtrip. "In his biography on the Web, Marlowe says that, and I quote, '[He] has further developed his relationships with the various congressional committees with jurisdiction over the issues that affect the firm's clients. In addition, he has established relationships with key members of the administration, the Departments of Transportation, Defense, Commerce, and Energy, as well as officials at independent agencies.' "

"That means he delivers PAC dollars the size of Montana."

Marlowe has a big staff of lobbyists. This indicated that Washington's culture of influence has gone on the Net. One member of the Marlowe team, Frank Moore, had been a staff director to a member of Congress and counsel to the Banking Committee, where he drafted over ten bills and fifteen amendments, and participated in legislation affecting financial institutions, housing, insurance, banking, and flood insurance. Marlowe and Company currently represent clients in those industries. Also at Marlowe are Scott Green, who had been a special adviser to Senate Judiciary Committee Chairman Joe Biden (D-Del.); Michael Nilson, former legislative aide to U.S. Rep. J. J. Pickle (D-Tex.); and Tom Bullock, ironically, an erstwhile project coordinator for the reform-minded Joint Committee on the Organization of the Congress.

One of the more sophisticated pioneers of Internet lobbying is IDI (Issue Dynamics Inc.), which bills itself as a Washington, D.C.-based PR firm. IDI began by flacking for the telecommunications industry and subsequently building bridges with consumer groups, schools, and universities. Their Web page states that IDI has become a "leader in bringing the tools of new communications and information technology to public policy discussions, debates, and decisions."

IDI is up front about the manipulative potential of the Internet. As soon as you access their Web page, you are told that the firm is the industry leader in "electronic advocacy on the Internet—how organizations can use this powerful new communications tool to conduct elements of a successful public affairs campaign, including lobbying, grassroots organizing, and mobilization."

IDI targets a number of major areas of Internet political activities, starting with electronic lobbying and building public support for clients' causes. "Using on-line techniques pioneered by

IDI, any organization can now electronically notify groups and individuals about pending legislation, make copies of the legislation available on an electronic bulletin board, provide sample letters expressing the organization's position, and direct Internet users to key committee members, including their e-mail addresses and telephone numbers.

"IDI has pioneered using the Internet as a tool for influencing public policy," the firm said. "We help our clients reach key government officials, industry leaders, and interest groups on the Internet with action alerts for constituent mobilization, electronic petitions, and interactive lobbying. We can identify potential allies, what areas of the Internet they visit, and make sure that your messages are seen.

"In addition, IDI is showing organizations how to generate electronic petitions. If a group opposes a new federal rule, for example, it can collect signatures from Internet users around the country and deliver the petition electronically to agency officials, members of Congress, and others. Increasingly, reporters and broadcast producers are also on-line and can be receptive to organizations providing information electronically, often resulting in media coverage of the organizations' positions on important issues.

"Like talk radio," IDI claimed, "the Internet can generate action quickly and directly."

"Great," sighed an already overworked Capitol Hill staffer whose office is drenched in stacks of computer-generated paper mail.

When next I reported to Roadtrip, he was beginning to sense the threat. "The day those scumbags put us out of business will be the day they perfect the traceless transfer of electronic cash. Because no matter what they do with their computers and their Net-gibberish, this is still a cash-and-carry business."

One person who has a sense of where it's all going is John Atkinson. Atkinson is a principal of the California firm of Silicon Media, Inc., which, unlike Green Lake and others, works only for Republicans. Atkinson, who runs the outfit's Washington office, was deputy communications director for Oliver North during the 1994 Senate campaign in Virginia. After designing the North campaign's computer system, Atkinson began to explore new ways to use high-tech campaigning. He probed the possibilities of message control through broadcast faxing systems, satellite feeds, and on-line services. More than anyone else, Atkinson is responsible for the high-tech legacy of the North campaign. Although not victorious, the North campaign was a groundbreaker from a technology management standpoint and a harbinger of things to come.

Atkinson sees the Internet as being in a developmental stage. "Last year, political campaigns began to appear on the World Wide Web," Atkinson said "These first attempts have been largely designed by college interns and young supporters who may know a lot about computers, but precious little about political communications. Many campaigns and political associations are using the World Wide Web simply as a repository for old press releases and speeches, with an occasional photo. But for delivering campaign messages and persuading voters, these sites are painfully inadequate. The audience is there, but it is up to the candidate to bring them the information they need in an interactive, multimedia format."

In good Internet fashion, I e-mailed Atkinson. He called an hour later.

"So what's happening out there?" I asked.

Atkinson is appropriately euphoric about the near future. "Nineteen ninety-six is going to be a teaser year," Atkinson predicted. "People will put up sites, but a lot of them will be volunteer efforts. You won't see much professional production in 1996. A lot of politicians and consultants see it as a toy, but it's changing rapidly. People who don't see that are going to get bit." Fellow expert Rod Kuckro agreed. "Nineteen ninety-six might be the 'beta' [test] year," he said, "but that doesn't mean it can't work for those who know how to use it."

Atkinson argues that the biggest benefit will be the ability to build a relationship with people who visit the home page. Such "visitors" can be reeled in as voters.

"Think of your standard thirty-second commercial," he said. "Now look at a World Wide Web page. For the fraction of the cost of a television commercial, you can go deeper and deeper—people can get into it and see what you're doing. You're also going to see more multimedia sites that are totally interactive."

"How so?"

"Unlike a commercial, the Web page is not in between a TV show," Atkinson said. "It *is* the TV show. People can choose what they want to see. It brings a lot more power into the hands of the voter."

Atkinson pointed out that a veritable "Washington Web" is in fact being woven quickly by members of Congress and their aides, the White House and executive branch, journalists, lobbyists, and hundreds if not thousands of individuals and organizations of every political persuasion imaginable.

Of course, this doesn't *necessarily* guarantee brilliant discourse. Writing in the *New York Times* on 30 August 1995, Barbara O'Brien, a moderator of a Usenet newsgroup, said, "The Net has become the world's bulletin board, on which anyone with a cause and a keyboard can spread his views. The result is a yeast of human craziness that is far more frightening than CD-ROM files of naked people." One of the groups that attracted O'Brien's attention was the zany Sovereign Citizens. They hold that people do not have to pay taxes and that the federal government has no jurisdiction in the states. Sovereign Citizens are further under the impression that since the 1867 Military Reconstruction Acts passed by Congress have never been rescinded, the United States is still under martial law.

One of the great things about the Net is that it gives people an outlet to chatter electronically about matters that the intellectual establishment and pundits reject as beneath their dignity.

They'll talk about anything on the Net. I decided to participate. Maybe the Net was the right forum to probe the mind of Newt Gingrich, as reflected in his new military thriller about a White House chief of staff and his Nazi mistress. It bugged me that everybody had ignored Gingrich's *1995*. Something about Newt's opus bothered me, and it wasn't just the awful writing. The collective silence from the family values crowd was more than interesting—especially in light of some weird tidbits from the novel that had been published in the *New York Times*. In case you missed them:

> Erika, the "beautiful and so very exotic mistress" of John Mayhew, the chief of staff, still pants, purrs, hisses, and sits "athwart his chest," all without ever using her "lethal pout." She twines the fur on his chest.... Explicit submission to her will could wait until he had composed himself. She was, after all, genuinely fond of him, and genuinely looked forward to further "games" in the context of their new relationship. Wait till he discovered the difference between feigned submission and the real thing. Between pretending to have no choice and having no choice. It would make a man of him. She wriggled with anticipation....

Now, can you imagine the outcry if Bill or Hillary had written a novel with explicit and exotic sex scenes? (Okay, okay, that's the story of Bill's life, but it doesn't answer the question. Why were the pundits and the think tankers so docile? You'd think they'd have had a field day.)

There was only one place to turn: the deep-dark, creepy-crawly holes on the margins of the Internet, lairs where nameless and unspeakable passions are traded 'round the clock....

In other words, exactly where Speaker Gingrich's novel belonged. This is the kind of topic that gets juices flowing on the

Internet. (Whitewater is another. On the Net, the words *Castle Grande* were thrown around long before any such references appeared in the newspapers. But back to Newt.)

In early March 1995, using my real name, I took a deep breath and posted my very first message to the Internet:

I am writing a book about Washington's political culture in the age of Clinton. Love him or hate him, one of the more fascinating characters in Washington today is House Speaker Newt Gingrich. To assist with research for the book, I am asking for Internet opinions about the sex scenes in his upcoming novel as reported in the *New York Times*. A major theme of my book is the importance of the human element in politics, and Gingrich's book may give us some clue as to how the mind of the person second in line to the presidency works.

Set during World War II and involving an illicit love affair between a White House chief of staff and an alluring Nazi spy, his book has several scenes described in the press as "racy."

In these scenes, the "beautiful and so very exotic mistress" is generally on top and giving orders (sitting "athwart his chest") and ("...genuinely looking forward to further 'games' in the context of their new relationship.... It would make a man of him.")

In your opinion, what kinds of observations can be made or conclusions drawn about a Speaker of the House who fantasizes about sex with dominant Nazi mistresses? Most of us have seen him on television and are familiar with his public persona. In your professional opinion, is there a shadowy side to the man who wrote the Contract with America? What other impressions do you have about Newt? Please send any opinions, facts, suspicions, or just plain rumors to "jackley@teleport.com" in the next two weeks. Thanks in advance for your help!

Deciding which groups to send it to was just as difficult. I examined most of the 5,000+ "newsgroups" available at the time, and decided to go for broke by sending it to the following:

✓ talk.rumors
✓ talk.politics
✓ alt.sex.bondage
✓ alt.politics.usa.newt-gingrich
✓ alt.politics.Clinton
✓ alt.personals.bondage
✓ alt.personals.spanking
✓ alt.sex
✓ alt.rush-limbaugh

A response from the Net sex professionals wasn't slow in coming.

Most of the respondents wanted Newt's telephone number. I considered it my duty to provide it. But I received replies—some insightful, some bizarre—from denizens of many other sites. All in all, it was great conversation.

"I think we need to find out if Newt has any of the alleged Nazi porno movies and that may answer our questions about him," one respondent sagely suggested.

A dominatrix from Greenwich Village was quite perceptive. "As a nonprofessional dominant," Mistress Autumn responded, "it is my considered, professional opinion that Mr. Gingrich has his little kinks and quirks just like the rest of America and just like you and I, my dear."

Alas, Mistress Autumn displayed a terrible snobbishness:

"It is a fact that his mother is white trash to the bone, what with calling Mrs. Clinton a 'bitch,' having the most egregiously bad taste to live in Pennsylvania, and then treating his sister Candace like a leper because Candy has the appalling stigma of lesbianism, and what's more, (eek!) Candy dares to be vocal about her 'perversion.' It is my experience that it is ever-so-difficult to take the white trash out of a person. Mr. Gingrich = White Trash? Highly likely. And White Trash tends to be of the 'Leave All Clothes On, Turn Off Lights, Before Coupling Hastily Only At Night' sexual persuasion... all the while fantasizing about the nastiest things...."

• • • •

ONE RESPONDENT was more cautious: "FYI: Newt's book is mostly ghostwritten, according to some recent stories I read. So if you're going to dig deep into his tecny, weeny little mind for character motivation (as disturbing a thought as that may be, given the Nazi dominatrix theme), I suggest you take it with a huge grain of salt."

• • • •

ONE RESPONDENT was woefully ill-informed: "I find it more interesting that he called Connie Chung a bitch. That's the thing that stands out most when I think of him," said Flintstone Girl.

• • • •

"AT LEAST we can be sure Newt isn't gay," said one Net pal, "because no gay man would dress so badly (he looks like a pork sausage in a sack) and have a dead albino squirrel asleep on his head (except maybe in a drag bar on Easter)."

• • • •

AND FINALLY: "He desires domination of the United States by a fascist style government although he would not necessarily be the 'man' in charge. Perhaps he might think of a newly invented Hillary as the Nazi Dominatrix of America. Whatever the reason, this Speaker gets a hard-on from powerful and dominating women. Perhaps he should mud wrestle with Margaret Thatcher?"

• • • •

And cyberspace is our future? Only on the Net, folks.

CHAPTER THIRTEEN

HTTP://WWW. SENATE.HOUSE. GOVERNMENT.?

ANDREW McMICHAEL is a twenty-nine-year-old graduate student at George Mason University in Washington's Virginia suburbs. He is working on his Ph.D. in history. He also has a strong background in computers, with the ability to program in multiple languages and run many different operating systems. As such, McMichael has become one of the Internet's gatekeepers as a moderator for the World War II newsgroup (**soc.history.war.world-war-ii**). Not surprisingly, McMichael sees the Net as a powerful tool to contribute to the good of society. At the same time, he is deeply concerned about its potential for contributing to the decline of public and private discourse. A registered Republican who sometimes votes Democratic, McMichael explained how political conversation has evolved on the net in the '90s.

"I've been on the Net for about four-and-a-half years now," he said. "I had my account through my university, but had initially heard about it through my brother. He had an account and told me about the newsgroups. Having used big bulletin board systems [BBS] for many years I initially saw the Net as a BBS where I could talk with people. When I got my initial account, I had to justify to the university why a history student needed an account—they didn't see the reason."

It was McMichael's interest in history that led him to become a moderator. "The first group I moderated was [and is] **soc.history.war.world-war-ii**," he told me. "Moderating takes the flames out of the groups and makes for a more academic discussion. I'm a big believer in moderation for history groups. The process is fairly simple: a user anywhere in the world posts an article to the newsgroup. Before it shows up it gets sent to one of the moderators [there are five of them] who reads it over and either approves it or rejects it. There is a charter that we set up that governs what can and can't be posted. We follow it very strictly [but not in the Civil War group]. The charter is always there for everyone to read so they know the posting guidelines. A moderator is like a little king, or set of kings, for the newsgroup. We change the charter for the group as we see a need, and ours is the only input that goes into changing it.

"Everyone has a say and is instantly validated through the electronic medium," McMichael continued. "We have grown into a society that trusts computers more than we trust ourselves. This is dangerous both physically and intellectually. Consider that everyone from a child to an adult can read and post to any newsgroup. We see these messages on our computers, and they are given an added validity because of the medium. And there are no editors to prevent falsehoods. The crypto-fascist and the anarchist are both given the same weight, electronically. It is up to the reader to sort them out intellectually. Not easy considering the authority we've given to the computer. We tend to be more intellectual than some groups because we can clearly explain our political philosophies."

"Do you have any sense about the ratio of pseudonyms to real names?"

"When Usenet participants were mainly comprised of academics, you rarely saw 'handles' because universities wouldn't allow it. The on-line services do, and so the trend is growing. Not good, in my opinion."

"What would be the impact from your standpoint on political discourse on the Net if everyone had to use his or her real names?"

"I'm all for people owning up to their beliefs, by using their real names, but I don't agree with those who say that people should be forced to use their real names. I think it runs contrary to what the newsgroups are about and what this country is about. Thomas Jefferson didn't use his real name in half his political writings during the Revolution. None of them did. However, if everyone were forced to use their real names I think that a lot of the extremism would fade. People would be too accountable and easily findable. Although many are proud of their extremism. In the World War II group we had to insert a clause in the charter specifically prohibiting posts about Holocaust revisionism, and in the [Civil War] group we had to add a clause that prohibits posts that blame Jews for the slave trade."

"I'd like to look at what you termed the 'instant validation' given to anyone who participates," I continued. "Is this good, bad, or indifferent?"

"I think that it is extremely bad. I don't think we validate the person, but the message in the form of words on our screen."

"How has it come to pass that we have conceded this authority to the computer?"

"We've been told for years that computers give us perfect answers if we feed the data into them," McMichael replied. "Think about it—if I entered the formula 47589*68752 into a computer and got back an answer, then I showed it to you and told you that the answer was different from what I calculated in my head— whom would you believe? Computers evolved into these omnipresent, omniscient machines that give us correct answers. The Internet has become a vast perversion of this. Not so much on the newsgroups, where there is someone right there in the next post to say 'Hey, you're full of it,' but on the Web.

"Web pages," McMichael went on, "are these huge, flashy, information 'machines' that tell us what we want to know. And there's no one there to say 'Hey, that's not right.' In an article I've just completed on this very subject, we found a Web page that says, in essence, that all of the nation's economic ills can be traced to the Banking Act of 1933. Kids today use the Web and the newsgroups to find information. On a newsgroup, as I said, it's not so bad as long as the kid is paying attention. But what happens when the kid comes across this? This is a minor example, of course.

"But what about if the kid looks at the neo-Confederate page that says that blacks were happy as slaves and supported the Confederacy during the Civil War?" McMichael continued. "And this info is juiced up by pictures, icons, and buttons, that give the page an air of authority like they'd get on the nightly news. Bad. Every month or so, on the unmoderated news-group, some grade or high school kid posts a message that says 'Hey, I've got to answer these ten questions for class. Can any-one help?' He'll usually get many responses, only a fraction of which are correct. Many people intentionally give false answers, saying that kids shouldn't rely on the Net for home-work. But where's the validity check? Well, if the kid keeps reading the newsgroup, he may see a message saying, 'That's not right.' Or maybe not. But on a splashy Web page there's no editor to cut out the BS."

"And are there any other areas where we have done so—in other words, what are the fundamental operating assumptions that are made without thinking (like instant validation) yet may have real implications later on?"

"We trust computers more than we trust ourselves, I believe,"

McMichael said. What was McMichael's experience with politics in the Web?

"It depends on which part of the Web you frequent," he said. "The interesting thing about the Web is that if you don't want to look at it, you won't. Conversely, if you want to read, say, some Republican mantra, you have to go seeking it out and know where it is. So politics, while growing, is still fairly sheltered."

Do politicians have any idea what's going on out there?

"Doubtful. But then that probably applies to many areas of the world. The Web in particular and the Internet in general are vast and confusing and operate by their own set of rules. I've been doing this for years now, and I'm not sure that *I* have any idea what's out there. It changes very rapidly."

I explained my findings to Roadtrip in a lengthy telephone conversation in September 1995.

"The Net," I pontificated, sounding somewhat sonorous after months of prowling cyberally, "has the potential fundamentally to transform fundamentally the way people and society communicate in politics and government."

"You may be right," he said with what I thought was a twinge of sadness. "And I sympathize with the original spirit of the Internet. I've done a little surfing myself by now. But you know what? It won't change human behavior, or what we do in this town or anywhere in politics. We'll figure out a way to do what we do even better. This will help us. You'll see attack Web sites during campaigns, just like you do on television today, and the kind of e-mail information warfare Kabay warned against will happen. Your Net people are asking grand questions about society and government. What they ought to be asking is, who's going to do the first Internet dirty trick? The first negative mass e-mailing? The first use of electronic cash to hide the identity of campaign contributors?"

"If it's good enough to be used," he finished, "it's good enough for this town to twist for its own purposes."

Let's see who else is on the political Net besides Newt and the sex pros. And there's only one way to find out: let's go surfing! Rev up your search engines, and dig around. Try it, you'll like it. A simple search on the Net yields a rich harvest of political sites, and the searching is easy if you know where to look. Here are some good places to start:

Webcrawler (http://webcrawler.com/). You'll get a large listing of sites, but it's unorganized and anything with the word "politics" in it will appear. It's a real crapshoot, and you can often be surprised.

Yahoo (http://www.yahoo.com/politics/). The best in the business so far as a political search engine, and it comes already organized by category.

All-in-One Internet Search (http://www.albany.net/~wcross/all 1www.html#www). A comprehensive set of search engines. If you don't already know which one you want to use, try here.

Netscape Netsearch (http://home/mcom/com/internet-search. html). Gives you Webcrawler and Lycos but not Yahoo.

To help make sense out of the gaggle of Web sites, I enlisted the help of an Internet pioneer named Dave Franks, one of the founding members of the state of Oregon's Internet system, a Democrat and all-around cool dude. Among others, Dave did the Web page for Monette trumpets, the best-in-the-world instruments played by Wynton Marsalis and other stars. Using our technical and political expertise, we devised a sophisticated computer ratings system based on weeks of effort and enormous mathematical calculations, which produced the following categories:

VERY COOL / Five Hillarys
COOL / Four Hillarys
JUST OK / Three Hillarys
LAME / Two Hillarys
SPAM / One Hillary

This rating is doubly negative because "One Hillary" is all Bill has, too. And who would have believed that zero Hillarys was anything negative?

A "Hillary," by the way, is our basic unit of measurement for the political effectiveness of any given political Web page. It is named in honor of her pink-suited performance on national television coolly denying any wrongdoing, moral or otherwise, in the Whitewater-related controversies, including making $100,000 in one day of commodities market speculation during the '80s that she and her husband so roundly denounced as the decade of greed.

The rating system does not make any value judgment about content, only its Net-worthiness and political effectiveness. Accordingly, the home pages for the Christian Coalition and the White House each received Five Hillarys and the coveted "VERY COOL" rating based on high levels of content, issues, links, ease of use, and effectiveness.

What do all the good sites have in common?

More than anything else, they understand John Atkinson's dictum that "the advent of the Information Age brings with it the ability to minimize reliance on costly and relatively limited methods of communication [mail, telephone, and television advertising].... At a single, easily accessible Web site you can inform the public clearly of your position on important issues, post a continuously updated schedule of major events, sign people up to your mailing list, and even solicit donations."

You can find a comprehensive set of political Web site links and ratings (and updates and corrections) in this book's Web page at http://www.teleport.com/~jackley/ratings.html. In the mean-time, here's a sampling of what brings home the Hillarys and what doesn't.

http://www.we.com/lgc/welcome.html A Layperson's Guide to Congress. Describes what Congress does and how it does it in very simple terms. Links to legislation, government documents, and a way to send a message to the members of Congress (although it doesn't say how they forward it). **COOL/Four Hillarys**

http://shango.harvard.edu/ The content of the JFK School of Government Home Page looks a bit weak from the initial page, but dig deeper. The Case Studies link brings you to the school's gopher server that contains lots of policy and politician case studies that are keyword searchable. **JUST OK/Three Hillarys**

http://www.lib.lsu.edu/gov/fedgov.html A list of federal agen-cies on the Internet. Not a list of politicians but a very complete listing of federal government agencies. Almost all have some kind of Internet presence, and this page can bring you there. We use it often, and it's a great index. **COOL/Four Hillarys**

http://www.webcom.com/~albany/rfk.html Robert F. Kennedy Democrats Warning: this page is graphic-intensive but these folks in Albany, New York, have some good links to content. Informa-tion about local, New York state , and national races and issues are here. The page links to Real Audio ™. **COOL/Four Hillarys**

http://www.ai.mit.edu/projects/iiip/kennedy/homepage.html Senator Edward Kennedy, the first member of Congress with a Web page. Graphics as heavy as his jowls after a rough weekend but with better design and speed than the Republicans or the RFK page. Content is limited to basically the same type of information as

Senator Bill Frist's page with the addition of links to the Massachusetts pages and information on the senator's intern program. **JUST OK/Three Hillarys**

http://www.vote-smart.org/ Project Vote Smart Politics on the Net should have the same thing as all good publications: content in the proper context. This site has it all, from issues and organizations to politicians, national information, local information, audio clips, humor, and a searchable data base. Need to find out how your representative voted on an issue dear to your heart? You'll find it here. And the graphics are clean and fast loading. How could you ask for more in a Web site? **VERY COOL/Five Hillarys** and runner up for the "Best of the Net."

http://www.cc.org/ Christian Coalition Professionalism, heavy content, and thoroughness mark this site. This Web site has information about conferences, articles from their magazine *American Christian*, and a congressional scorecard that rates how representatives have voted in relationship to their agenda. The site covers local as well as national issues. It could use better and more balanced links. **VERY COOL/Five Hillarys**

http://www.house.gov/default.html House of Representatives Home Page. A long time coming, and Newt gets big-time kudos for doing what the Democratic leadership should have done years ago. Good links. Compare this one with the White House's! **VERY COOL/Five Hillarys**

http://www.aflcio.org/ AFL-CIO. Graphics download slower than changes in union shop rules. You'll find press releases, policy statements, a boycott list, and an AFL-CIO news site consisting mostly of press releases (the first one on 9/13/95 is titled "Union Is Only Worker Hope"). Because of clunky construction, you really have to work to find out what they have to say. **LAME/Two Hillarys**

http://dgsys.com/~cgriffin/ Cyber Politics. Done by a Chip Griffin in the D.C. area. Good links and you can sign up for regular updates about political developments on the Web. This political resource directory has over two hundred sites in politics and government and is great. The directory of other directories is particularly thorough (**http://dgsys.com/~cgriffin/direct.html**). **VERY COOL/Five Hillarys**

http://thomas.loc.gov/ The Thomas site at the Library of Congress. Quick graphics, and it does exactly what it was designed to do: provide quick, easy, and current information on legislation in the U.S. Congress, the *Congressional Record*, text of bills, bill status, e-mail address of Congresscritters, and more. **VERY COOL/Five Hillarys**

http://www.whitehouse.gov/white_House/eop/first_lady/-html/Hillary_home.html Hillary's Home Page is a lot like her: slow to download, gets on a roll, and doesn't shut up. The first thing to download is her picture and then some audio files. We haven't had the courage to listen. It also features the least-visited site on the entire Internet called "Health Care Speeches by the First Lady." This Hillary is **SPAM!**

http://www.ca-democratic-party.org/chameleon.html "Pete Wilson Exposed," a hit page by the California Democratic party. It's worth looking at this page once so you can see why they lost California to Pete. The graphics take forever to download. And put on your hip boots because you're going to do some deep wading and slogging through this one. A good opportunity blown. Bob Squier, where are you? **LAME/Two Hillarys**

http://www.house.gov/democrats/ The U.S. House of Representatives Democratic Leadership—we thought that was an oxymoron these days, but this page is solid (although we'll pass on the opening item, the Message from Chairman Gephardt; pass the Seconal, and fast). Constituent service, the party line, stuff for students and seniors, FAQs (Frequently Asked Questions). One link is "Who Are the Democratic Leaders?" Before you say, "That's one hell of a good question," check this page out. Too bad the Republicans haven't done one, yet, but maybe if you control the House you don't need a Web page. Not! **VERY COOL/Five Hillarys**

http://www.cs.dartmouth.edu/~crow/whitewater/whitewater.html Whitewater Scandal Home Page. Everything you wanted to know about the scandal, including **http://www.cris.com/~dwheeler/n/whitewater/deadfoster**, which is where you subscribe to the "Dead Foster" mailing list. **VERY COOL/Five Hillarys**

And now the drum rolls, please....

http://www.netview.com/polinet/ The Political Network. Terrific, surpassing even Yahoo for completeness. Graphics download fast and are very well organized. Links by state, party, ideology, presidential campaign, student, organization, even top political stories around the clock via media link—you name it, they have it. If you could access only one political site, this is it. **VERY COOL AND OUR ALL-AROUND WINNER of the coveted Six Hillary Award**, the only one of its kind.

Politics, of course, needs news and the news media for fuel. We didn't rate these, but some are better than others.

http://www.yahoo.com/headlines/current/politics/ News from Reuters On-Line. One of the best.

http://www1.trib.com/NEWS/ Another excellent news site. Reuters, Associated Press, *New York Times*, ABC, CNN, superb international links. One of the best.

http://www.cudenver.edu/psrp/news.html News and documents.

http://www.sfgate.com/examiner/index.ht *San Franciso Examiner* home page. A good way to get the news without having to see the picture of the hyperambitious and insufferable Washington bureau chief, Chris Matthews, former chief of staff to former House Speaker Tip O'Neill, and one of the Clinton administration's grinning cheerleaders.

http://www.well.com/news.html News links from the Well; very good.

http://server.berkeley.edu/herald/ The Internet Herald, or in its own words, the "The Hip Gen X Web Zine." Pu-lease! Hip this, buddy.

http://www1.trib.com/news/ Great international links.

Here are the wild and wooly Usenet groups. Enter at your own risk!

✓ talk.politics.misc
✓ alt.politics.clinton
✓ alt.politics.elections
✓ alt.politics.radical-left
✓ alt.politics.usa.congress
✓ alt.politics.usa.republican
✓ alt.politics.usa.newt-gingrich
✓ alt.current-events.clinton.whitewater

[Note: All Web sites are subject to change without notice by the organizations and people who maintain them. Our ratings were done in late 1995. You can find a current, up-to-date set of political site listings and ratings no matter when you read this book at **http://www.teleport.com/~jackley/ratings.html**.]

As with most previous campaign techniques, such as television, direct mail, and use of correct spelling and grammar, the Democrats and liberals—as we noticed in the previous chapter—are for the most part behind Republicans and Independents on the Net—except in Congress, where Democrats have jumped to a surprising lead in access, resources, and overall content.

"The Democrats are into it," said the aforementioned Atkinson of the North campaign. "Even though the Web is trending 48 percent Republican, they're putting up a fight for it. The Republican leadership in the House has only two sites, and there's nothing there. Contrast that with Gephardt's Democratic leadership site. But as soon as the Republican leadership figures it out, they'll get it."

For the time being, however, Atkinson rates the Clinton White House Web site as one of the best. "They had very good marketing," he said. "In April [1995], you couldn't open an Internet magazine without seeing something about the White House being on-line. They had pros do it, too, which is not always the case. Phil Gramm's Web page was put together by a bunch of college students."

Which is where, apparently, the first great Internet mistake of Campaign 1996 took place. College Republicans did Gramm's Web page, but forgot that the Web can take you anywhere, and will. An enterprising reporter found a link at the bottom of the Gramm page to the commercial provider of the Internet site, and after a few clicks found one of the largest-ever sites of Internet pornography. Such is life on the Net.

So I left behind the world of the Internet and its prophets and zealots, its language of societal transformation and potential for political disruption, and continued my journey. The advent of companies like IDI, that lurk about the Internet discussion groups and America Online chat rooms, silently recording the conversations and identities of the participants, marked the first real shadow cast over the Net.

"You know, it's time to reach for your zipper when Michael Kinsley shows up," Roadtrip cracked. The former co-host of "Crossfire" show has left the network to start an Internet magazine for Microsoft Corporation. "The King of Spin has arrived," Roadtrip said, "and with an entourage."

"Is he the Sally Quinn of 1996?" I asked.

Roadtrip allowed as how that was an intriguing thought, and he would e-mail me any further comment.

Attack Web sites and e-mail wars are expected momentarily. The age of cyberspace innocence is over, if there ever was one. The politicals have found fresh game, and they twist their snares and they watch and they listen and their minds turn, figuring out how to use it for that one more political edge over their rivals in the grand game of Washington.

Now it was time to slip into a world where there is no pretension of innocence lost, ever: the culture of Clinton, which, underneath the hoopla, was just as sleazy and manipulative as it had accused its Republican predecessors of being, and then some.

"You're going from the world of invisible bytes and e-mails and clean machines and computers, and across the Bridge of Sighs into the Inferno," warned Roadtrip. "Be ready."

CHAPTER FOURTEEN

THE CULTURE
OF CLINTON

Bev Bassett [Clinton-appointed Arkansas bank regulator] is so fucking important....
If we fuck this up, we're done.
—White House Deputy Chief of Staff Harold Ickes at a Whitewater
damage control team meeting to get Bassett's story straight,
from the notes of former White House communications
director Mark Gearan at his Senate Whitewater
testimony, 21 February 1996

Cynicism is our enemy.
—President Bill Clinton, 17 February 1996

THE WHITE HOUSE STAFFER had had a bad day, and it was time to unload:

"You just wouldn't believe what it's like here right now," the staffer sighed shortly after New Year's in 1996. "There's a complete disconnect going on. Stephanopoulos, Panetta, Morris, Ickes, the president himself sometimes—a lot of them act like they're on top of the world, that they're winning the budget battle on Medicare, and they got Gingrich and the congressional Republicans on the defensive, turning the corner on this or that. Then the meeting or the conversation breaks up, and they return to what they're doing, and the sense of impending gloom and doom sets in. Ickes turns red and purple and shrieks a lot, especially at things in the newspaper. He seizes the paper like it's some kind of captured rodent, and he's trying to shake its neck off. Sometimes I think he's trying to sound like Clinton. Stephanopoulos is one of the worst because he always has to have an audience for his feelings. And he's scared of Ickes because Ickes has Hillary's ear. Panetta is the organization man trying to keep George and Dick Morris from killing each other. As if anyone would care. This damn Whitewater thing is just hanging over everything and everyone. It has the damp, foreboding sense of a nineteenth-century manor house novel. One thing after another, day after day after day. And the greatest fear around here is the great unknown because there isn't a person on this staff who in his heart of hearts doesn't believe that the Clintons are capable of lying to all of us—or even to themselves—about what's going on and the great 'what happened' question.

"Every day we reinvent the search for enemies," the staffer continued. "It's the press, a right-wing conspiracy, those damn congressional Democrats, you name it. We have an internal barometer around here to tell how crazy things really are. Stephanopoulos has kept a back-channel communication to [House Democratic Leader Richard] Gephardt and the Gephardt operation ever since he started on the Clinton campaign. This is separate from the official go-betweening he does. George talks to Gephardt three ways. There's the official message—the 'check with Gephardt' instruction. There's the casual, unofficial talk he tells Panetta about and that stuff that goes on at Gephardt's Democratic message meetings. Then there's his back-channel. And the worse things get, the more he pisses and moans to Gephardt. And he thinks nobody knows. But a lot of the little people here know, and word gets around in curious ways. We talk about it. Who's playing who? George? Gephardt? What are they trading off each other? Certainly nothing that's helping Clinton. I hear it's deep dish—political dish, legislative tip-offs, handwringing over the way Hillary's dragging the presidency down, whatever hell Hillary is raising that day. George is a true believer, all right—in George and George's feelings. You mark my words. George is one of the Clinton administration's canaries. I even heard the rumor that intermediaries have quietly touched base for him with literary agents about a future book. I guess it wasn't enough for him to spill his guts to whoever wrote *Primary Colors*. I don't know who did it, but the language and the maudlin soul-searching of the narrator has George Fucking Stephanopoulos written all over it from cover to cover. He even told the press that there was a conversation in that novel that had only taken place between him and the president. So are we supposed to be surprised that it shows up in print? No, because George talks to his friends and one of them wrote a book. He barely survived all his blabbing to [*Washington Post* editor and author Bob] Woodward [in the book *The Agenda*]. We'll see what happens to him now. Ickes was blowing a cork over the book, yelling at everyone about loyalty, and from what I heard, Hillary would just as soon tank George's ass tomorrow.

"All the chickens are coming home to roost around them," the staffer shuddered, "the dark things from Arkansas, the president's indiscretions, Hillary and her people. If I ever have to see Susan Thomases dress down another United States government official with that insufferable attitude of hers, I don't know what I'm going to do."

But we both knew what he was going to do. No matter how bad it is, working in the White House—any White House, even Jimmy Carter's or Bill Clinton's (and probably Warren Harding's or Ulysses Grant's White House too)—is the ultimate political rush, the biggest of the big leagues, the Real Show. It's money in the bank. You'll relive it for the rest of your life. (There's always some washed-up, has-been drunk at the end of any Washington bar who begins every conversation with the phrase, "When *I* was in the White House....") But in Clinton's White House, the sense of short-term political advantage is accompanied by long-term anxiety.

This has everything to do with the Fall of Politics. In the personages of Bill and Hillary Clinton converge the Twilight of the

Enlightenment and the Fall of Politics. They have profited handsomely through both, but they have paid dearly, too. Bill Clinton was the perfect candidate for the Twilight of the Enlightenment. He was the master of the art of public self-confession—he felt our pain, and he had the perfect story to "share": the alcoholic stepfather, the abusive background; Bill Clinton was a one-man case study of the self-help and recovery movement. Even more so than Ronald Reagan, Clinton had the knack for telling the story that hit the heart; it was accompanied by the Elvis overbite and the downcast eyes. Clinton ran not so much a traditional presidential campaign as a national recovery program—or a revival. Clinton's biblical rhetoric, especially Job and redemption, took full advantage of the ebbing away of rational discourse, while his emotive, personal stories vied with position papers for a place in the national dialogue.

In the process, Bill and Hillary Clinton personified the Fall of Politics. Despite their best attempts to convince us otherwise, they are separated from—they have fallen from—the rest of America and its values. They do not share our values. They are not the first or the last, and certainly not the only ones in Washington politics to separate themselves from us. But they were the first president and co-president in modern memory to convince us, if only for a moment, that things would be different. Wracked by economic uncertainties, the public in 1992 was so hungry for someone who was not part of Washington's Permanent Political Culture that the Clinton campaign bloomed, despite Gennifer.

Now they have had to live with what they did to get here. Once in the White House, the facade began to fall apart. The political disasters of early 1993 did more than bog down the Clinton co-presidency. They revealed that the president and his wife operated on a set of cultural characteristics that comes right out of the Fall of Politics. And there is, in fact, an identifiable culture of Clinton that affects the administration's every move. This culture is actually composed of a number of building blocks that reflect various permutations of the Fall.

"The problem that the Clintons just can't shake," Roadtrip said, "is that the political disasters in the first year—the botched nominations, the betrayal of the middle class platform of the campaign and the emergence of 'fooled-you' liberalism, the proposed energy tax increase, and all the rest—showed the country that they were incompetent. Then came Whitewater, which showed they were crooked."

"I can see that disturbs you greatly," I said.

"We were worried a little bit with all that anti-Washington rhetoric during the campaign," Roadtrip admitted. "But then the transition appointments started being announced, and when Clinton spent that first night in town after the election with [superlobbyist] Vernon Jordan and a bunch of contributors, a giant sigh of relief could be heard from one side of the Beltway to the other. Sure, he brought some TCFs with him, but they handled the dirt from Arkansas, not national policy. Clinton wasn't that stupid." (A "TCF" was Roadtrip's term for the Arkansas contingent in the White House, standing for "Toothless Cousin Fuckers.")

"Ron Brown got in hot water right away and survived," a former White House staff explained. "Zoe Baird and Kimba Wood didn't raise a dime for Clinton. Brown brought it in by the truckload."

In place of genuine morality, we get nitpicking about what's politically correct; PC matters have slowed down the administration's ability to react quickly. For example, the administration floundered for months in 1993 because of the systematic exclusion of otherwise qualified white males from various essential slots. The attempt to find a qualified woman for U.S. attorney general consumed valuable time and only ended when an obscure Florida prosecutor named Janet Reno surfaced. The emphasis on hiring by gender may have been one reason why by the end of February 1993, President Clinton had submitted only thirty formal nominations for the 290 jobs that require Senate confirmation. To get around this, many departments were, in effect, hiring temps.

White House Press Secretary Dee Dee Myers dutifully informed the press that the delay was caused by "casting the net wider than in the past and getting a diversity in terms of race and geography and background."

"There wasn't even a cosmetic attempt to find the so-called 'most qualified person' regardless of politically correct characteristics," said Roadtrip.

It affected policy as well as politics. "One of the huge problems the Clinton administration has is in policy formulation," said Gary Jarmin of the American Freedom Coalition, who has great sense for a conservative. Jarmin continued, "And it's unique because of the role the First Lady plays in policy formulation. In the past, people would say OK, here's a foreign policy recommendation to the president. OK, we've got to run it by Anthony Lake, Warren Christopher, Defense, the agencies—get input, then present it to the president. What's unique in this administration is that the policy process suddenly becomes perverted because you have to consider not just what those players want, but the Hillary factor as well."

Jarmin explained why developing policy took so long in the administration. "People are not going to put their careers on the line for a policy, with all the hard work and ego involved," he said, "when it's all going to be for naught because Hillary, without taking the time to study the issue, is going to kill it."

The culture of Hillary slows down the White House… and as a result, the entire nation. The watchword becomes anxiety. Anxiety about our standard of living, wages, and… jobs.

It was "the economy, stupid" in 1992, but in 1996, it's simply "jobs." IBM announced layoffs of 60,000 in July 1993 (and 85,000 through 1995), followed by GTE's layoff notice of 17,000 in January 1994. Chemical/Chase Manhattan slated a workforce cut of 12,000 in the summer of 1995, and AT&T announced in January

1996 layoffs of 40,000 employees—a full 13 percent of its staff. The layoffs underscored broader economic uncertainty. According to the Census Bureau, median family income, adjusted for inflation, was $38,782, 1 percent below 1991. The Bureau of Labor Statistics released figures on 29 January 1996 that showed the average weekly earnings of 80 percent of Americans who are "production and non-supervisory workers" fell 18 percent after adjusting for inflation between 1973 and 1995.

Many families have not made up their losses from the 1990–91 recession. And by the spring of 1996, layoffs and job security had shoved aside the budget debate in the consciousness of normal Americans, dominating the national conversation from the evening news to the water cooler.

The White House's public confidence and optimism is purely a front. Behind the scenes, they share our apprehension about the economy. "There's a delicate balancing act going on here between the economy, political combat with the Republicans, and the threat of Whitewater," said a source with access to Oval Office discussions. "On the economy, he's got to take spot credit—California, good numbers, whatever—while dodging the claim of overall responsibility for an economy that could go belly-up at any point, particularly if a major stock market correction takes place. The political outlook is better now that Republicans are carving themselves up unless Buchanan's success pushes Powell back into the race. And Whitewater—well, that's the tough piece of the puzzle that's out of the staff's ability to control in many ways."

Clinton, however, sees a way out, according to my sources.

"Clinton is following a clear script," another White House staffer said in February 1996. "We [the source's friends on the staff] call it the ultimate scam because (1) it's so transparent, (2) it's downright blasphemous, and (3) it has more than a fair chance of working."

I was intrigued.

"They clearly blew the first two years, flat-out. Oh, sure, there's the reinventing government blah-blah, and the reeling off of the paper accomplishments blah-blah, and all the rest of the blah-blah, but basically the first half of the first term flat-out sucked. The biggest disasters were Hillary's policies—and that means public image, health care, Whitewater, commodity profits, the whole works—and the president's character—indecisiveness, screwing your friends, losing golden opportunities, and the rest.

"So what does he do? The pundits call it running against himself and his record, but what he's really trying to do is script his own redemption. It's biblical, and it's on purpose. That's what the last several months have been all about. The telephone call to Ben Wattenberg about values and appearing reflective and repentant over past mistakes? The 'funk' episode, even though he nearly blew it there? The sudden discovery of a line in the sand over Medicare, where the real policy differences with the Republicans are, generally speaking, minor? It's got nothing to do with policy and everything to do with redemption. Morris isn't writing strategy memos. He's rewriting Job, and Bill Clinton is the main character. Even the State of the Union speech was laced with the subtle language of redemption. It took weeks of polling and message-testing to get each of those lines honed and perfected. We put Reagan's polling operation to shame."

Hillary, too, is being redeemed, but in a different way. "Project Betty Crocker," as a friend on the White House staff termed it, is an effort to transform Hillary from health czar to cookie czar, and was conceived sometime between the November 1994 elections and January 1995.

Hillary's new image was the subject of an intense internal debate. There are two versions of the debate. One, Hillary was violently opposed to it and fought it tooth and nail, but caved under pressure and the president's desire that she do it. Or two, she was merely disgusted at the prospect of being portrayed as a traditional woman, but decided in the end it was no worse than sticking up for Bill over Gennifer Flowers and Paula Jones.

The end result was the same, and after some last-minute historical research into the public images of previous First Ladies, Project Betty Crocker was formally launched early in 1995. According to White House sources, most of the administration's political shamans had a crack at it: James Carville and Paul Begala, Leon Panetta, Doug Sosnik, Margaret Williams, and others. After several rounds of discussions (with and without Hillary's participation), the plan included the following elements:

- A series of calculated public events that linked Hillary personally and especially visually to photo-ops, issues, and causes associated with traditional views of women and First Ladies in particular.
- An equally calculated effort to keep her out of the public eye in connection with anything having to do with public policy other than politically safe women's issues.
- Strict orders to White House staff and administration officials prohibiting the mention of her name to the media in conjunction with legislative policy. "Nothing was written down," said a political appointee from Capitol Hill who was at an executive branch agency, "but our [Cabinet] secretary spelled it out in our staff meetings loud and clear." A White House staffer commented, "We were told point-blank by Ickes that he never wanted to see a media story again about how smart a lawyer she was."
- Her progress would be measured in the regular White House tracking polls used to craft the president's legislative and communications efforts, and fine-tuned accordingly.

"Hillary, by the way, made it perfectly clear, and often huffily so, as if she was trying to make a deliberate point, that she would retain her existing power and authority behind the scenes," said a staffer familiar with the discussions.

The result was a systematic promotion of stories and events to rebuild her image, piece by piece. The White House realized that such a makeover would not happen overnight, and a timetable was developed to take them into early 1996 to coincide with the presidential reelection effort. The capstone would be the publication of her book, *It Takes a Village and Other Lessons Children Teach Us*, and the accompanying warm-and-fuzzy book tours. White House strategists were salivating at the prospect of a string of photo ops of Hillary with children throughout early 1996. The strategic approach was to test the waters in early 1995, lie as low as possible during the Contract with America debates in Congress, then promote her new newspaper column mid-year and take advantage of breaking opportunities that could showcase her new role.

She came out of the chute with a *New York Times* interview published 10 January 1995, in which she used the same self-reflective, redemptive technique her husband had fine-tuned so well. She blamed her image problems on her own "naivete" and expressed regret that her efforts on health care reform had been "badly misunderstood" and "taken out of context." Her audience? A group of women writers, including Ann Landers, who covered style, gossip, and the First Lady's social functions.

"That's not exactly *ABC News Nightline*," remarked Roadtrip. "She has the 'Fonz problem'—she just can't ever come right out and say she was *wrong*." The *Times* story, in fact, referred to a similar effort in the 1992 campaign to make her appear more feminine and traditional. Back then, it was called the Manhattan Project.

"And they both dealt with a bomb that could blow up in your face at any time," Roadtrip laughed.

The next major move was made in mid-February 1995, in a story on the front page of *USA Today*'s Living Section about her efforts to redecorate the Blue Room in the White House. Roadtrip noticed the "I-can't-believe-I'm-doing-this" look on her face in the accompanying photograph before I did. Hillary is standing to the left of a redecorated chair, which she holds in her right hand, and the look of complete contempt on her face is priceless. All things considered, she should have looked happier. June 1995 was a big month for Hillary. She received extensive press coverage for criticizing the use of sex in advertising aimed at children, urged help for families, and even impressed conservative columnist Cal Thomas by her appearance with Mother Teresa in support of adoption.

Her "touchy-feely" newspaper column hit about a hundred papers in the third week of July 1995; it reflected on her role as First Lady (and did not mention, either, that she was a smart lawyer or the "p" word [policy] at all). The next month featured an ABC television special on landmarks associated with notable American women, in which she talked about the impact of Susan B. Anthony.

The biggest moment of the remake: Beijing.

On 5 September 1995, the First Lady arrived in China for the UN World Conference on Women. The press photograph shows her descending from the plane with U.S. Ambassador Madeleine Albright trailing several steps behind. Roadtrip took one look at the photo and cracked, "What can possibly be going through the mind of Madeleine Albright as Hillary steps off the plane with a triumphant strut—a professional diplomat and accomplished national security strategist having to walk three paces behind a someone who's so utterly clueless and yet thinks she knows it all."

As Hillary attacked China as a country that abused women and had tried to suppress discussion of the issues at the conference, Ambassador Madeleine Albright nervously buttonholed reporters to reassure them that Mrs. Clinton's speech did not reflect a new China policy. On the other hand, the *New York Times* called Beijing Hillary's "finest moment in public life." "There was jubilation in the East Wing and a sigh of relief in the West Wing," a West Wing staffer reported. "We thought she had really turned the corner on all her PR problems."

But will Hillary be able to keep on playing the new role? "Mark my word," said a White House staffer, "there's a seething volcano inside. She can do this Betty Crocker thing for only so long—she's pent-up—if he's reelected, she's going to be hell on wheels in the second term."

But there was still one problem, and it quickly became an enormous one: Whitewater.

Missing billing records from the First Lady's Arkansas law firm had been sought by federal prosecutors for two years. Somehow they suddenly and mysteriously turned up in the White House, and before you could say "It Takes a Village," Hillary Rodham Clinton became the first First Lady in U.S. history to be subpoenaed in a federal criminal probe.

"It takes a village, all right," Roadtrip said. "A village idiot, that is."

More problems arose. The book tour spun out of control as soon as it was launched. There was criticism for not naming Washington writer Barbara Feinman as a co-contributor to the book. Instead, Mrs. Clinton insisted that the work was all hers. Feinman had clearly done extensive research, editing, and writing. Then there was the content, a skewed "multiculturalism" that teaches that every other culture on the planet is superior to the West's, and most especially to that of the United States.

(The Romans may have conquered my distant ancestors in Gaul and Britain, but I do not hold that against Italians.)

"No, actually, it warmed our hearts. We were worried. Some of us were actually starting to believe that *they* actually believed that moral crap."

After talking to the usual suspects in Democratic circles—low friends in high places, White House staffers, congressional sources, lobbyists, consultants, administration officials—a thumbnail portrait of the culture of Clinton emerged:

It is manipulative. It orchestrates events, conversations, even public gestures to a degree unimagined by the average person. "All

White Houses script their presidents," Roadtrip said, "but what sets this one apart is the sheer brazenness of it all, and the degree to which it is out in the open." All presidents manipulate, but from Abraham Lincoln to Franklin Roosevelt to Ronald Reagan, great presidents have done it on behalf of a vision of the nation and a core set of values. For Clinton, that cupboard is long bare from a never-ending stream of constant reinventions, as he has struggled to move poll numbers instead of a nation. His so-called trilogy of personal speeches in the summer of 1995 asked us to accept the argument that the baring of his political soul (yet again) was in itself worthy of praise. As the *Wall Street Journal*'s Al Hunt remarked in July 1995, "This is a White House that plays the angles, too often with a finger up to test the political winds, leaving many voters baffled as to what, if anything, this president stands for."

It is self-destructive. From believing that the public would forget about the middle class tax cut and the promises to crack down on welfare reform, the Clintons have repeatedly proven themselves to be too smart by half. And for the first time in the modern era, a president's sex life and personal ethics have come to dominate the national conversation. How many other presidents are at the other end of a 1-800 number where for twenty dollars plus shipping and handling you can listen to him talk on tape for an hour to his mistress?

It has betrayal as its core value. We've already seen what the Clintons have done with the campaign promises of 1992—the "new" Democrat of "reciprocal responsibility," welfare reform, a middle class tax cut, and smaller government. On the personal level, the wake of the culture of Clinton is clogged with the flotsam and jetsam of careers and people from Little Rock to Washington who were dumped when convenient. And in the policy arena, congressional Democrats up for reelection in 1996 are still outraged over Clinton's comments that the tax hike was really their baby.

It is vindictive. Neither Clinton can respond to critics or policy opponents without questioning their motives, engaging in personal attacks, or seeing conspiracies. Hillary Rodham Clinton in December 1993 blamed a vague conspiracy for political attacks based on the president's alleged use of Arkansas state troopers to help arrange "dates." During the Travelgate brouhaha, *Newsweek*'s Meg Greenfield noted the Clintonian propensity to "publicly accuse others of criminal conduct or ethical improprieties without observing even the most elemental requirements of due process and fair play."

This vindictiveness permeates the administration. Consider Mike McCurry's remark during an official briefing that Newt Gingrich would like to see senior citizens die: "...they'd like to see the [Medicare] program just die and go away. You know, that's probably what they'd like to see happen to seniors, too, if you think about it."

"That was scripted from start to finish," said a source in the White House political shop. "McCurry, Panetta, Ickes, Hillary, the president—they all agreed it would be a great hit to force Gingrich to deny he wanted to kill seniors."

In a similar tactic, McCurry used metaphors from recent incidents of terrorism to describe legitimate policy differences with opponents. Immediately after the November 1995 assassination of Israeli prime minister Yitzhak Rabin, for example, White House chief of staff Leon Panetta charged congressional Republicans with a "form of terrorism" in the budget battle. After the Amtrak sabotage in Arizona, McCurry equated Republican spending cuts with taking "the bolts out so the train could run off the track."

It was irrevocably wedded to Washington's culture of influence from the beginning. The Clintons were always part of the national Permanent Political Class of Washington. Both campaign and administration were peopled by pillars of the Democratic establishment, so much so that Clinton's promise to "change the way Washington does business" is ludicrous.

It is arrogant and elitist. In a pathetic attempt to emulate John F.

Kennedy, the Clintons assembled a smug yuppie meritocracy that confused credentialism and cleverness with real accomplishment and wisdom. "Punks in regalia," Roadtrip called them. They continue to annoy the nation with their claims to a higher civic and moral authority, even as the floodwaters of scandal lap ever nearer. At a time of ever-increasing economic uncertainty and a revolt against the liberal culture, the Clintons in January 1996 still could not resist leaving budget gridlock and a shut-down federal government behind to take in yet another Renaissance Weekend, where over a thousand of their fellow yuppies in law, academia, the media, business, and government convened to soul search, jog, and hug.

"We did our damnedest to get them not to go," bemoaned a White House aide after the Clintons had departed. "It's just so stupid. The self-important image just kills us, all while the government is shut down.... Jesus."

More than anything else, it is the culture of Hillary, not the culture of Bill, that dominates the administration. To borrow a description from the computer world, Bill is the interface, but Hillary is the operating system. Her ego, her sense of mission and self-importance, and her ability to generate fear—all these warp the administration. *She* clears the important speeches, the public announcements, and the government policy initiatives. She strains official resources with her insistence on being treated organizationally as a co-president—the briefings, the research, the memos, and the accompanying bowing and scraping. She picks her battles and refuses to budge, from insisting on a woman U.S. attorney general to refusing to compromise over her heath care reform scheme. "She expects to be treated as an equal source of presidential power," a West Wing staffer reported, "and she gets it."

"The culture of Clinton has changed in some respects over the course of the presidency," a White House staffer said. "You had the initial disorganization, followed by the Graduate School Seminar and the First Dorm Room. Panetta led the Revolt of the Grown-Ups and punks like Stephanopoulos were exiled. Next month, it might be something else. But the core never changes, and that core is Bill and Hillary. Especially Hillary."

• • • •

As usual, Roadtrip had the last word.

"And there you have it," Roadtrip summarized. "That's the culture of Clinton: dominated by Hillary, without any core values or beliefs other than survival and political correctness, consumed by crises of their own making, and watching Whitewater march toward them like zeroing-in howitzer shells. And even if they win the election, what will they have really won? What will they have really changed except themselves?"

"Roadtrip," I replied, "we're on our own."

EPILOGUE

THE IMAGE OF THE DECENT public servant is largely a myth when it comes to Washington, D.C. Any exception is nothing more than an accidental truth. The very concept of decency implies that there is something short of revolutionary change a person can do to make things better. The Fall of Politics does not mean doing away with politics, but it does mean a new realism about the business of government. Before we can achieve real political reform, we must reform our illusions. That could be difficult because despite Bill Clinton's desperate attempts to distance himself from his observation that the country was in a "funk," he was right. We are in a funk about the system, and no amount of "reinvention" is going to cure that. Voters rebel against a special interest-dominated Congress, and African American jurors acquit black defendants in criminal trials not because they believe the defendants are not guilty, but to punish a system they distrust and fear. The militia movement slowly gathers strength in the rural West. Americans of all races and income levels, having lost faith in government's ability to protect its citizens, now arm themselves in record numbers. You see America's loss of faith in demographic patterns, too. A September 1995 Census Bureau report showed that fewer and fewer Americans are moving. This is a historic shift. "We have always been a country based on optimism and new frontiers," Dr. Walker D. Burnham, a government professor at the University of Texas. He told the *New York Times*, "This seems like a different world, one that looks more like a frozen river than a fluid stream."

Washington politics is not a journey into the light, but a descent into an underworld. Washington politics is culture, a fusion of its own and reflective of the cultures of the American public. Politicians are, fundamentally, cultural creatures who react to cultural pressures. And politics is, as we have seen, a decidedly different culture from those in the rest of America.

Proclamations to the contrary, Bill Clinton is as tragically separated from the real values of real people as any other politician. And, proclamations to the contrary, Republicans are no different. Like their Democratic counterparts, they too sell access to special interests and engage in the same hunt for campaign dollars. Even more profoundly, however, the new Republican forces share the same belief with the old congressional Democrats and Bill Clinton that politics is the appropriate vehicle by which to transform the country. Republican politicians behave as creatures in the culture of politics exactly as Democratic politicians do. They have different priorities, issues, and constituencies, but their systemic actions are the same. To use a term from the computer world, they share the same basic operating system. Clinton and Gingrich differ only in direction of action and distribution of spoils: both would use the national government to reshape the country; both would use the force of the national government to compel certain public and private behaviors; and both see their personal brand of politics as salvationary for themselves, their institutions, and their country.

The culture of Clinton reflects not only his personality and character, but the depth of his personal Fall into Politics. Washington's institutions show no sign of anything but the Fall, from the antics on the Hill (Rep. Mel Reynolds's sex crime conviction, Newt Gingrich's ethical blind eye, former House Speaker Tom Foley's pathetic new role as a lobbyist) to the gaseous punditry of the Washington circuit and the twisted fears and anxieties that dominate the culture of Clinton and the schemer crowd.

The Fall of Politics shows that not only is Washington politics not redemptive, but those within the political culture need to seek redemption. This is part of the solution: you must force yourself to realize that you are not part of a noble calling but of an inherently tragic one, of a world rife with inherent flaws and a fundamental cultural separation from the rest of the country.

Nothing will change Washington politics, ever. To change Washington and what the political culture represents would be to change human nature itself. I offer no instant solution to the Fall of Politics. There are, however, hints that we could manage and structure a way of conducting politics that recognizes the Fall. In terms of specific solutions, I see the need for term limits. Only term limits—and limits on all levels, including local, regional, and state—physically remove the individual from the political culture, or at least the part of it where the individual can exercise power and make decisions on behalf of and in the name of the public. A third party may be the next logical and natural step from the standpoint of the current political dynamic, but it too will be composed of human beings like thee and me and will operate in the shadow of the Fall as do the rest.

There are no climactic battles for the soul of the political culture. Power is behind the Fall of Politics, power and what the temptation of power can do to a person. Some wounds never heal, and politics is one of them. Power is the canvas, and Clinton and Washington are merely the colors.

Politics is culture, and politics is human. More than anything, Washington politics is tragedy.

INDEX

ABC News poll, 34. *See also* Polls
  and surveys
A.C. Nielson Company, 148
Activist government, 71
Ad campaigns. *See* Negative cam-
  paigning
Ad Hoc PAC Coalition, 108
Adams, Brock, 126
AFL-CIO Web site, 173-174
Ainsworth, Dr. Scott, 133-134
Akin, Gump, Strauss, Hauer, and
  Feld, 107
Albany, New York, 172
Albright, Madeleine, 189
Alexandria, Virginia, 51
"Alliance for Reinventing Govern-
  ment," 36
Almanac of American Politics, 87

America: What Went Wrong?, 5
American Enterprise Institute, 123,
  135
American League of Lobbyists, 112
Andrews, Wright, 104, 112
Anthony, Beryl, 111
Armey, Dick, 106
Aspen Summit: Cyberspace and the
  American Dream II, 153
Atkinson, John, 157-159, 177

Baird, Zoe, 92
Banking scandal, 56-57
Barlow, John Perry, 147
Barone, Michael, 87
Bartlett, Donald L., 5
Bassett, Bev, 179

BBS. *See* Bulletin board systems
Begala, Paul, 65, 67
Beijing, China, 189
Better than Sex, 35
Birnbaum, Jeffrey, 54
Black, Gordon, 85
Bolt counterfeiting, 19
Bonior, Dave, 23
Boren, David, 109-110
Bradlee, Benjamin, 43
Breast cancer, 125, 127
Britano, Dr., 124
Brookings Review, 119
Brown, Ron, 71-72, 89, 92-93
Browner, Carol, 49
Broyles, William, 52
Bryant, John, 114
Budget battle, 61-62
Budget Day, 79
Bulletin board systems, 166
Bullock, Tom, 156
Bureau of Labor Statistics, 185
Burger, Tim, 111
Burnham, Dr. Walker D., 196
Bush, George, 5, 10-11
Bush Administration, 55

C-SPAN, 59-60
California Democratic party Web
    site, 174
Campaign finance reform, 92, 108-
    110, 113-114. *See also* Political
    action committees
Cannon, Angie, 7
Card, Andrew, 82
Carter, Jimmy, 32
Carville, James, 4
Census Bureau, 185, 196
Center for Public Integrity, 108
Center for Responsive Politics, 71,
    104-105
Century 21 Real Estate, 103

Checking scandal, 56-57
Christensen, Jon, 102
Christian Coalition Professionalism
    Web site, 173
Cisneros, Henry, 64
Clay, Michelle, 104
Claybrook, Joan, 54, 142
Clinger, William F., 89
Clinton, Bill
    anger over political diaries, 46
    budget battle, 61-62
    culture of Clinton politics, 190-194
    election of, 62-63
    Gennifer Flowers affair, 72-73
    new role for Hillary, 64-67
    policy formulation, 184
    political appointees, 31-35
    political disasters, 182-183
    political nominations, 183-184
    promise of moral politics, 9-10
    redemption of, 186
    reinventing government, 36-38
    scandals, 63-64
    sex stories, 95
    State of the Union speech, 86-90
    timber summit, 76
    Washington's political culture and,
        67-73
    White House staffers, 179-181
Clinton, Hillary Rodham, 6, 58-59
    on Gennifer Flowers affair, 73
    home page, 174
    new image, 186-190
    new role for, 64-67
    political diary, 46-47
    public's early perception of, 63
    role in policy formulation, 184
    spirituality, 83
    Third World visit, 65-66
Clinton White House Web site, 177
CNN poll, 34. *See also* Polls and
    surveys
Coleman, Ronald, 28, 56

Coltec Industries, 91
Computer information age, 81. *See also* Internet; World Wide Web
Congress bashing, 12-14, 140, 143
Congressional corruption, 16-30
Congressional junkets, 141
Congressional Record, 16, 19, 20, 21
Consultants, 31-32, 154-157. *See also* Lobbyists
Contract with America, 106
Cook, Charles, 122, 136
Corridor (broadcasting company), 94
Corruption in Congress, 16-30
Cote, Neil, 122
Council on Competitiveness, 27
Counterfeit bolts, 19
Crawford, Ron, 117
Credentialistas, 36
Cultural conservatism, 128
Customer service standards, 38
Cutler, Lloyd, 45, 73
Cyber Politics Web site, 174
Cyberspace, 148. *See also* Internet; World Wide Web

"Datahead," 13, 34
Davis, Bob, 22-27
Decentralization, 151
DeLay, Tom, 106
Democratic Club, 28
Democratic Leadership Council, 87
Democratic National Committee, 6, 38
Deutch, John, 82-83
Diaries
   political, 43-47
   sex, 101
Discourse on the Origins of Inequality, 75
DLC. *See* Democratic Leadership Council
DNC. *See* Democratic National Committee

Dodd, Christopher, 95-96
Dole, Bob, 105-106
Dole, Robin, 103
Dondero, Russell, 131-132
Dowd, Maureen, 69
Duberstein, Ken, 144-145

e-mail. *See* Internet
Economic issues, 184-185
Eisenach, Jeffrey, 153
Eisenstat, Stuart, 32
Enlightenment, 80
Espy, Mike, 64, 82
Estrich, Susan, 108
Ethical issues, 129, 131
"Expert opinion," 136

"Fact-finding" trips, 112-113
FDIC. *See* Federal Deposit Insurance Corporation
Federal agencies listing, 172
Federal Deposit Insurance Corporation, 89
Feinman, Barbara, 190
First International (communications company), 94
Flowers, Gennifer, 72-73, 126
Foley, Kim, 18-19
Foley, Thomas, 5, 53, 86-87, 92, 107
Foster, Henry, 48
Franklin, Elaine, 101
Franks, Dave, 170
Freshman representatives, 90-91
Fund, John, 106

Gallup poll, 34. *See also* Polls and surveys
Game theoretical model, 133-134
Gans, Curtis, 122
Gearan, Mark, 179

Gejdenson, Sam, 110
Gelerntner, David, 81
Gephardt, Richard, 180-181
Gergen, David, 59
Gibbons, Clifford, 104
Gift ban, 114, 141
Gingrich, Newt, 68
  budget crisis, 61-62
  campaign reform, 113-114
  1995 book, 160-164
  PACs and, 105, 106
Gold and Liebengood, 111
Gore, Al
  on cynicism, 64
  Harvard Commencement Day
    speech, 68
  reinventing government, 36, 37, 38
Government Reform and Oversight
  Committee, 102
Gramm, Phil, Web page, 177
Green, Scott, 156
Green Lake, 154
Greenfield, Meg, 192
Grofman, Dr. Bernard, 122
Guth, James, 131

Haldeman, Bob, 43-44
Hamilton, Lee, 118-119
Harris, Mr., 20
Hart, Gary, 96
Hartwell, Robert, 21
Hastings, Alcee, 114-115
Health care reform task force, 58-59
Health care system, 7
Heritage Foundation, 123
Hill, Anita, 125-127
Hill and Knowlton, 57
Hill Rat, 12, 17, 117-118, 120
Hillary's home page, 174
Hollings, Ernest, 27-28
Hostetter, Lynn, 154
House banking scandal, 56-57

House Budget Committee, 102
House Government Reform and
  Oversight Committee, 89
House of Representatives home
  page, 173
Howard, Philip, 36
Hunt, Al, 191
Hyde, Henry, 106

Ickes, Harold, 89, 179-180
IDI. *See* Issue Dynamics Inc.
Information Age, 81. *See also* Internet; World Wide Web
Inside Edition, 15-17, 29
International news Web links, 176
Internet, 147. *See also* World Wide
  Web
  Aspen Summit, 153
  description of users, 150-151
  effect on politics, 151-152, 167, 169
  growth of, 148
  lobbyists and consultants, 154-157
  messages on Gingrich book, 160-
    164
  moderators, 166
  political sites, 170-177
  reinventing government site, 37-38
  terms for, 149
  use of pseudonyms, 167
The Internet Herald, 176
Issue Dynamics Inc., 156-157
*It Takes a Village and Other Lessons
  Children Teach Us*, 188

Jarmin, Gary, 184
JFK School of Government home
  page, 172
Job losses, 184-185
Joint Committee on the Reorganiza-
  tion of Congress, 118-119
Jones, Paula Corbin, 52

Jordan, Vernon, 4
Junkets, 141

Kabay, Dr. Mich, 151-152
Kantor, Mickey, 50
Keisling, Phil, 49
Kennedy, Robert F., Democrats
  home page, 172
Kennedy, Ted
  sex stories, 95-96
  Web page, 172-173
Kinsley, Michael, 178
Kitzhaber, John, 36
Kotkin, Joel, 88
Kuckro, Rod, 150, 158-159
Kuhn, Thomas, 120

Lawyer-lobbyists, 11-12. *See also*
  Consultants; Lobbyists
Layoffs, 184-185
A Layperson's Guide to Congress,
  172
Lee, Donald, 20, 23, 29
Lee, Harris, and Carlson, 20
Lerner, Michael, 83, 122, 128-129,
  131, 132
Lewis, Charles, 108, 142
Library of Congress Web site, 174
Lobbying reform, 141
Lobbyists, 11-12, 56-57, 103-113.
  See also Consultants;
  Washington's political culture
  number of, 39, 88-89
  use of the Internet, 154-157
The Lobbyists, 53-54
Lowi, Ted, 122-123, 129-131
Luntz, Frank, 106

Makinson, Larry, 71, 104
Mankiewicz, Frank, 57
Mann, Dr. Thomas, 117-119, 127-128

Marlowe, Howard, 91, 155-156
Marlowe and Company, 154-156
Matalin, Mary, 4
Maxfield, Meredith Stewart, 102
McCurdy, Dave, 87
McCurry, Mike, 36, 48, 192
McGrory, Mary, 46
McMichael, Andrew, 165-169
McPherson, Harry, 31
Meagher, Matt, 19-29
Merida, Kevin, 117
Microsoft Corporation, 178
Miller, Ellen, 142
Minorities, 125-126
Moderators, 166
Moore, Frank, 156
Mutual Life Insurance Company,
  104
Myers, Dee Dee, 184

Nabisco. *See* RJR Nabisco Holdings
  Corporation
NABPAC. *See* National Association
  of Business Political
  Action Committees
Nader, Ralph, 109, 111-112
National Association of Bolt Distrib-
  utors, 19
National Association of Business
  Political Action
  Committees, 111
National Computer Security Associ-
  ation, 151
National Institute of Standards, 27
"National Performance Review," 37-
  38
Negative campaigning, 121-122
Neumann, Mark, 91
New Deal, 123
New Democrat, 88
New England Mechanical Trader's
  Inc., 19, 29

New Romanticism, 81-82
News Web sites, 175-176
Newsgroups, 149, 150, 165-168
Newsweek poll, 3-4
Nilson, Michael, 156
1995, 160-164
Nixon, Richard, 35
Nofziger, Lyn, 42, 58, 87
North, Oliver, 158

O'Brien, Barbara, 159
Official portraits, 82
Olson, Walter, 36
Oregon's Pacific University, 131-132
O'Reilly and Associates, 148
Ornstein, Dr. Norman, 117, 119,
    135-145
Osborne, David, 35-36

Pacific University, 131-132
Packwood, Bob, 46, 101-102, 117,
    126
PACs. *See* Political action committees
Paxon, Bill, 91
Permanent Political Culture, 4, 14
Perot, Ross, 3-4, 10
"Perspective on the 104th Con-
    gress," 145
"Pete Wilson Exposed," 174
"Plum List," 32-33
Pokios, Perry, 110
Political action committees, 71, 90-
    91, 104-105, 142. *See
    also* Campaign finance reform
Political diaries, 43-47
The Political Network, 175
Political power, 78, 86. *See also*
    Washington's political culture
Political scientists, 120-134
Polls and surveys
    distrust of federal government, 7

early confidence in Clinton, 34
government control, 7-8
Internet users, 148, 151
term limits, 106
voter preferences, 3-4
Polsby, Dr. Nelson, 124-125, 136
Popkin, Samuel, 123
Portland State University, 79
Portraits, 82
Powell, Colin, 4
POWERNET, 155
Press secretaries, 79
Primary Colors, 181
Prime Rib restaurant, 22-25
"Prof quote," 136
Project Betty Crocker, 186-187
Project Vote Smart Politics, 173
Public choice, 120
Public service standards, 38

Rasmussen, Scott, 107
Reagan, Nancy, 58
Reinventing Government, 35
Reinventing government, 36-38,
    79-80
Religion, 129, 131
Reno, Janet, 89
Rice, Donna, 96
RJR Nabisco Holdings Corporation,
    4
"Roadtrip," 28-30, 38-42
    on campaign finance reform, 113-
    114
    on Clinton political disasters, 182-
    183
    on Clinton's State of the Union
    address, 90
    on Congress bashing, 12-14
    on the Internet, 147, 169
    on lobby reform, 112
    on new role for Hillary Clinton,
    66-67

on Norman Ornstein, 142
on political diaries, 45-46, 49-50
on political scientists, 121
on polls, 34-35
on quote by Harry McPherson, 31
theory on Washington's political
  culture, 85-94
on Washington political system,
  54-58
Robert F. Kennedy Democrats home
  page, 172
Roberts, Barbara, 36
Roger, Paul, 11
Roll Call, 29
Rostenkowski, Dan, 144
Rota, Robert, 144
Rousseau, Jean-Jacques, 75
Rubin, Robert, 92
Rumor-mongering, 151

San Francisco Examiner home page,
  176
Savage, Gus, 126
Scholarly journals, 124-127
Schulze, Richard, 21
The Scientific Revolution, 120
"Scoop," 93-94
Senator Edward Kennedy Web page,
  172-173
Sex diaries, 101
Sex in Washington, 95-102
Shadegg, John, 102
Sherill, Martha, 63
Sierra Club, 109
Sikorski, Gerry, 57
Silicon Media, Inc., 157-158
Silicon Media Web page, 151
Skaperdas, Dr. Sergio, 122
"Slick," 15-29
Smith, Linda, 91
"Soft" money, 70, 88, 90, 109
Souder, Mark, 90

The Soul of Politics, 5
Sovereign Citizens, 159
Spiritual issues, 129, 131
Sportsmen's Caucus, 102
State of the Union speech, 86-90
Steele, James B., 5
Steiner, Josh, 44-45
Stephanopoulos, George, 44-45, 50,
  53, 180
  arrogance of, 4-5
  political beginnings, 41-42
Steve (surveillance expert), 21, 22,
  24, 26
Stockmeyer, Steve, 108-110
Strossen, Nadine, 46
Surveys. *See* Polls and surveys

Tallon, Robin, 27-29
Tax issues, 7
Term limits, 106-107, 197
Term Limits Leadership Council,
  107
Third World countries, 65-66
Thomas, Clarence, 125-127
The Thomas site at the Library of
  Congress, 174
Thompson, Hunter S., 6, 18, 35
Thurber, James, 124
Timber summit, 76
Times-Mirror survey, 7

UN World Conference on Women,
  189
U.S. House of Representatives
  Democratic Leadership Web
  site, 175
U.S. Term Limits, 106
USA Today/CNN/Gallup poll, 34.
  See also Polls and surveys
Usenet political groups, 176

Wall Street Journal, 106
Wallis, Jim, 5, 81
Washington Post, 20
Washington Post/ABC News poll,
  34. *See also* Polls and
  surveys
Washington Web, 159
Washington's political culture, 67-
  73, 76-79, 85-94, 106,
  195-198. *See also* Lobbyists
Web page. *See* World Wide Web
Weber, Vin, 105
Weingarten, Reid, 45
White House Web site, 177
Whitewater investigation, 47, 190

Whitewater Scandal home page, 175
Whitten, Jamie L., 103
Wilkey, Malcolm, 47
Williams, Linda, 128
Williams, Patricia, 114-115
Williamson, Marianne, 83
Woburn, Massachusetts, 19
Women's issues, 125-127
Wood, Kimba, 92
World War II newsgroup, 165-167
World Wide Web. *See also* Internet
  author's home page, 145, 171-172
  description, 149
  effect on politics, 152-153, 158-159
  Web pages, 168